T0366380

GESCHLECHT III

Geschlecht III

SEX, RACE, NATION, HUMANITY

Jacques Derrida

Edited by Geoffrey Bennington,
Katie Chenoweth, and Rodrigo Therezo

Translated by Katie Chenoweth
and Rodrigo Therezo

The University of Chicago Press
Chicago and London

The University of Chicago Press, Chicago 60637
The University of Chicago Press, Ltd., London
© 2020 by The University of Chicago
Published 2020
Printed in the United States of America

29 28 27 26 25 24 23 22 21 20   1 2 3 4 5

ISBN-13: 978-0-226-67746-0 (cloth)
ISBN-13: 978-0-226-68539-7 (e-book)
DOI: https://doi.org/10.7208/chicago/9780226685397.001.0001

Originally published in French as *Geschlecht III. Sexe, race, nation, humanité*
© Éditions du Seuil, 2018.

Library of Congress Cataloging-in-Publication Data

Names: Derrida, Jacques, author. | Bennington, Geoffrey, editor. | Chenoweth, Katie, editor, translator. | Therezo, Rodrigo, editor, translator.
Title: Geschlecht III : sex, race, nation, humanity / Jacques Derrida ; edited by Geoffrey Bennington, Katie Chenoweth, Rodrigo Therezo ; translated by Katie Chenoweth, Rodrigo Therezo.
Other titles: Geschlecht III. English
Description: Chicago : University of Chicago Press, 2020. | Includes bibliographical references and index.
Identifiers: LCCN 2019027816 | ISBN 9780226677460 (cloth) | ISBN 9780226685397 (ebook)
Subjects: LCSH: Heidegger, Martin, 1889–1976. | Sex—Anthropological aspects. | Sex—Political aspects.
Classification: LCC B3279.H49 D483813 2020 | DDC 193—dc23
LC record available at https://lccn.loc.gov/2019027816

♾ This paper meets the requirements of ANSI/NISO Z39.48-1992 (Permanence of Paper).

CONTENTS

PREFACE

This edition presents the reader with a text that seemed lost forever.[1] Scholars were long astonished by a remarkable gap in the project on Heidegger and *Geschlecht* that Derrida planned in the 1980s: a series of four essays forming a more or less coherent whole, yet the third part of which we were denied until

1. From the start of this preface, we would recommend that the reader consult the final pages of "Heidegger's Hand (*Geschlecht* II)," in Jacques Derrida, *Psyche: Inventions of the Other*, vol. 2, ed. Peggy Kamuf and Elizabeth Rottenberg (Stanford, CA: Stanford University Press, 2008), 51–62—where Derrida provides a "very cursory sketch" of the "five foci" around which he confined himself to indicating, "in just a few minutes" at the end of his lecture at Loyola University in Chicago in March 1985, the "principal concern" of *Geschlecht III*—as the true point of entry to the "hundred or so pages" of *Geschlecht III*. We also refer the reader to the remarkable work of David Farrell Krell, who has more recently contributed significantly to drawing philosophers' attention to the mystery of *Geschlecht III*; see David Farrell Krell, *Phantoms of the Other: Four Generations of Derrida's "Geschlecht"* (Albany: SUNY Press, 2015); and Krell, "One, Two, Four—Yet Where Is the Third? A Note on Derrida's Geschlecht Series," *Epoché: A Journal for the History of Philosophy* 10:2 (2006). See also Françoise Dastur, "Heidegger and Derrida on Trakl," in *Phenomenology and Literature: Historical Perspectives and Systematic Accounts*, ed. Pol Vandevelde (Würzburg: Koenighausen & Neumann, 2010), 43–57; and Peggy Kamuf, "The Other Sexual Difference," in *Book of Addresses* (Stanford, CA: Stanford University Press, 2005), 79–101.

now.[2] Although Derrida himself never published the third *Geschlecht* text, he named it—as such or indirectly—multiple times during the two last decades of his life. As the publication of *Geschlecht IV* in 1994 already makes clear, Derrida never abandoned the desire to write *Geschlecht III*, even if that desire was deferred as often as the will to fulfill it was expressed. This desire even "magnetized" all the other *Geschlechter* before or at the moment of their birth, as Derrida tells us from the opening words of *Geschlecht I*, in a footnote placed after the title:

> This essay [. . .], like the following one ("Heidegger's Hand [*Geschlecht* II]"), will have to content itself with sketching in a preliminary fashion an interpretation to come in which I would like to situate *Geschlecht* in Heidegger's path of thought. In his path of writing as well—and the imprint, or inscription marked by the word *Geschlecht* will not be innocent here. I will leave this word in its own language for reasons that should impose themselves on us in the course of this very reading. And it is certainly a matter of "*Geschlecht*" (the *word* for sex, race, family, generation, lineage, species, genre), and not of *Geschlecht* as such: one will not so easily clear away the mark of the word ("*Geschlecht*") that blocks our access to the thing itself (the *Geschlecht*); in that word, Heidegger will much later remark the imprint of a blow or strike (*Schlag*). He will do so in a text we will not speak of here but toward which this reading is heading, and by which, in truth, I know it is already being magne-

2. It could be claimed that the entirety of the four *Geschlechter* indeed constitute Derrida's most sustained confrontation (*Auseinandersetzung*) with Heidegger, an interlocutor Derrida privileges in his deconstructive reading of the history of Western philosophy. "*Geschlecht* I: Sexual Difference, Ontological Difference" and "Heidegger's Hand (*Geschlecht* II)" appeared in *Psyche: Inventions of the Other*, vol. 2, while "Heidegger's Ear: Philopolemology (*Geschlecht* IV)" appeared in French as an appendix to *Politiques de l'amitié* (Paris: Galilée, 1994), 343–419, and in English in *Reading Heidegger: Commemorations*, ed. John Sallis (Bloomington: Indiana University Press, 1993), 163–218.

tized: "Die Sprache im Gedicht: Eine Erörterung von Georg Trakls Gedicht" (1953), in *Unterwegs zur Sprache* (Pfullingen: Neske, 1959); "Language in the Poem: A Discussion on Georg Trakl's Poetic Work," in *On the Way to Language*, trans. Peter D. Hertz (New York: Harper & Row, 1971).[3]

This last text is mentioned several times in *Geschlecht II*, where Derrida explains that he had dedicated to it a "hundred or so pages" in the course of a seminar titled *The Ghost of the Other*—the first in a series of four seminars given under the general title *Philosophical Nationality and Nationalism* (1984–88). These "hundred or so pages" on Heidegger's essay on Trakl do correspond in part, as Derrida himself says, to a thirty-three-page text that he did not read at a conference organized by John Sallis at Loyola University in Chicago in March 1985. The lecture as Derrida delivered it would go on to become "Heidegger's Hand (*Geschlecht II*)"; the text he decided to forgo delivering "should have been titled '*Geschlecht III*'": "I will not give this part of my lecture, which should have been titled '*Geschlecht III*' and whose (typed) manuscript has been photocopied and distributed to some of you so that a discussion of it might be possible. I will confine myself then to a very cursory sketch of it."[4] At first glance, then, it seems legitimate to identify this "manuscript" as the whole of *Geschlecht III*. And yet, given the way Derrida describes it as "a first French version, incomplete and provisional," we might suspect that *Geschlecht III* in fact corresponds to the "hundred or so pages" of the seminar rather than to an "incomplete," thirty-three-page typescript. The latter indeed constitutes what Derrida refers to, on the last page of the typescript, as a "transcription" of only a *part* of the "hundred or so pages" (or "roughly a hundred pages") of *Geschlecht III*: "The transcription of the seminar had to stop here, for lack of time. Five sessions, or roughly a

3. Derrida, *Psyche*, 2:7 (translation modified).
4. Derrida, 2:51.

hundred pages, remain to be transcribed. Please do not circulate this sketch of a rough draft: *provisional and incomplete*!" If we compare the Loyola typescript and the text of the seminar where *Geschlecht III* begins—namely, the end of the seventh session of the 1984–85 seminar—we may better understand the meaning of the words "transcribe" and "transcription" here: what is at stake is a minimal revision or editing of a text initially destined for those in attendance at the first seminar Derrida gave at the EHESS (École des Hautes Études en Sciences Sociales) in Paris. A comparison of these two versions of the beginning of *Geschlecht III* reveals that the differences are limited for the most part to typographical and stylistic corrections, with several exceptions that we will indicate when called for. This practice of "transcribing" a text initially written for his seminar so as to transform it into a work published outside of that immediate context was common for Derrida; the particular case of *Geschlecht II* is exemplary for us here.

Indeed, the published version of *Geschlecht II* is itself a "transcription" of the two sessions (the sixth and nearly all of the seventh) that immediately precede *Geschlecht III* in the 1984–85 seminar. This published "transcription" sticks very close to the original, such that it would be difficult here, too, to locate any significant differences. This is what for us justifies the decision to publish *Geschlecht III* as such, even though Derrida himself never did, for reasons that are unknown. In addition to the fact that Derrida himself names *Geschlecht III* at least twice, still thinking of it when *Geschlecht IV* was published almost ten years later (announcing *Geschlecht III* there as a "forthcoming essay"), one can assume that the complete transcription of *Geschlecht III* would also have stuck very close to the seminar—which justifies, then, this posthumous publication of the Loyola typescript *followed* by the "hundred or so pages" of the 1984–85 seminar as indeed the text that "should have been titled '*Geschlecht III.*'"

* * *

Beyond these philological considerations, it would also be necessary to illuminate a motif belonging to the order of thought. We have already mentioned that *Geschlecht III*—and the reading of Heidegger's essay on Trakl that is developed there—"magnetized" Derrida's whole project on Heidegger and *Geschlecht* from the beginning. Before spelling out the meaning of this magnetization, let us comment more generally on this word—or, rather, this "mark"—"*Geschlecht*," which provides the general title or subtitle for these four texts. "*Geschlecht*" is an untranslatable German word, a highly charged and attractive polysemic amalgamation that no doubt magnetized Derrida. As he reminds us, the signification of this word radiates out toward semantic valences so diverse that "one will not so easily break through [this mark] to the thing itself," to the *Geschlecht* beyond the mark "*Geschlecht*," as it were. All the more so given that, in itself, this word *remarks* the mark, in what ties it to the *Schlag* (the blow, strike, or imprint) of every *Geschlecht*, as Heidegger recalls in his essay on Trakl. Sex, race, family, stock, branch, generation, lineage, species, type, people, nation, humanity:[5] these meanings make "*Geschlecht*" rather conducive and appealing to Derrida's thought, which strives to speak of that which Heidegger would, to all appearances, have had trouble addressing—namely, the political and sexual themes that Heidegger no doubt considered too ontic and derivative to merit discussion or thought, and which, in any event, he tends to pass over in silence. "*Geschlecht*" would be the exception to this rule in Heidegger, and we may understand why Derrida—thinker of writing and the mark, of sexual difference and the democracy to come—found himself "magnetized" by this politico-sexual dimension of *Geschlecht*. Let us try now to discern more precisely what this magnetization

5. The reader of *Geschlecht III* will have noticed that the subtitle we have given to this volume (*Sex, Race, Nation, Humanity*) is intended to "translate" *Geschlecht* into the meanings that are most relevant for Derrida's reading.

may have entailed. It is itself polarized around the two poles of the politico-sexual axis we have just named.

First, the sexual pole: in an interview with Christie Mc-Donald from 1982—just one year before *Geschlecht I*—Derrida speaks of his desire and his "dream" of a sexual difference (that is, a *Geschlecht*) beyond the binary opposition of man versus woman. Even if this latter difference seems to "set off 'the war between the sexes,'" sexual difference determined in this way erases itself from the start, according to Derrida:

> One could, I think, demonstrate this: when sexual difference is determined by *opposition* in the dialectical sense (according to the Hegelian movement of speculative dialectics, the necessity of which remains so powerful even beyond Hegel's text), one appears to set off the "war between the sexes"; but one precipitates the end with victory going to the masculine sex. The determination of sexual difference in opposition is destined, in truth, for truth, to erase sexual difference. Dialectical opposition neutralizes or sublates difference.[6]

In the immediate context of this interview, Derrida suspects Heidegger and Levinas of this type of phallogocentric neutralization that "according to a surreptitious operation [. . .] insures phallocentric mastery under the cover of neutralization."[7] "Against" such a sexual opposition—what would it mean to be "against" opposition?—Derrida dreams of a sexual difference "beyond binary difference":

> This indeed revives the following question: what if we were reaching here, what if we were approaching here (for this is not reached like a determined location) the zone of a

6. Jacques Derrida and Christie V. McDonald, "Choreographies," trans. Christie V. McDonald, *Diacritics* 12:2 (Summer 1982): 72 (translation modified).
7. Derrida and McDonald, "Choreographies," 72.

relation to the other where the code of sexual marks would no longer be discriminating? A relation that would then not be a-sexual, far from it, but sexual otherwise: beyond the binary difference that governs the decorum of all codes, beyond the opposition feminine/masculine, beyond bisexuality as well, beyond homosexuality and heterosexuality which come to the same thing? As I dream of saving the chance that this question offers, I would like to believe in the multiplicity of sexually marked voices, in this indeterminable number of blended voices, in this mobile of non-identified sexual marks whose choreography can carry the body of each "individual," traverse it, divide it, multiply it, whether he be classified as "man" or as "woman" according to the usual criteria.[8]

According to the terms of this interview, Heidegger would be situated, to all appearances at least, on the side of the philosopher who can only repress the Derridean dream in the name of a supposed sexual neutrality that has in truth always declared "victory [for] the masculine sex."

Yet it is unquestionably something else that "magnetizes" the beginning of Derrida's project on Heidegger and *Geschlecht* in 1983. In *Geschlecht I*, Heidegger seems to play a much more equivocal role than that of simply one phallogocentric philosopher among others (indeed, the word "phallogocentric"[9] nowhere appears in this text)—all the more so given that it is precisely Heidegger's thought that now seems to lead toward "the other sexual difference" Derrida dreamed of in the

8. Derrida and McDonald, 76.

9. Derrida first proposed this term, to the best of my knowledge, in "Tympan," first published in French by Éditions de Minuit in 1972; then in English in Jacques Derrida, *Margins of Philosophy*, trans. Alan Bass (Chicago: University of Chicago Press, 1982), ix–xxix. See also Jacques Derrida, *Glas*, trans. John P. Leavey Jr. and Richard Rand (Lincoln: University of Nebraska Press, 1990); and Derrida, *Spurs: Nietzsche's Styles/Éperons: Les styles de Nietzsche* (Chicago: University of Chicago Press, 1981).

interview with Christie McDonald just one year earlier. At the end of *Geschlecht I*, Derrida writes the following about a passage from a lecture course Heidegger gave at Marburg in 1928:

> This order of implications opens onto the thought of a sexual difference that would not yet be sexual duality, difference as dual. As we have already observed, what the lectures neutralized was less sexuality itself than the "generic" mark of sexual difference, the belonging to one of the two sexes. Hence, in leading back to dispersion and multiplication (*Zerstreuung, Mannigfaltigung*), might one not begin to think a sexual difference (without negativity, let us be clear) that would not be sealed by the two? Not yet or no longer sealed? [. . .] The retreat of the dyad is on the way toward the other sexual difference.[10]

Without embarking on a detailed discussion of Derrida's reservations about this "order of implications" in Heidegger—it is a question of the Heideggerian gesture that still takes the risk of deriving sexuality, even "with the force of a new rigor," by subtracting it from the existential structures of *Dasein* (which does not mean that this gesture might not *also* allow for the "retreat of the dyad" and the path toward the other sexual difference)—let us underscore that the "magnetization" that motivated Derrida to write four texts on Heidegger and *Geschlecht* emerged out of the "dream" that Derrida seems, up to a certain point, to share with Heidegger.[11] A dream always haunted by what Derrida refers to as the "implacable destiny" or the "merciless closure" of sexual binarism from which the dream protects us, perhaps:

> Of course, it is not impossible that the desire for a sexuality without number can still protect us, like a dream, from an

10. Derrida, *Psyche*, 2:26 (translation modified).
11. Derrida, 2:22.

implacable destiny which seals everything for life with the figure 2. And this merciless closure would come arrest desire at the wall of opposition, we would struggle in vain, there would never be but two sexes, neither one more nor one less—the tragedy would have this flavor, a contingent one all told, that we would have to affirm and learn to love instead of dreaming of the innumerable. Yes, perhaps; why not? But where would the "dream" of the innumerable come from, if it is a dream? Doesn't the dream itself prove what it dreams of—which must indeed be there in order to make us dream?[12]

* * *

Geschlecht III is no doubt the *Geschlecht* that most makes us dream of this other sexual difference beyond or on this side of the binary one. The reading promised in the footnote to *Geschlecht I* concerns Heidegger's 1953 essay on Trakl that Derrida describes in *Geschlecht III* as "a grand discourse on sexual difference" in which "an entirely other experience of sexual difference" is promised.[13] It would be necessary, of course, to specify what *division* is at stake, rather than letting one thinker simply fall into the shadow of the other. We must limit ourselves here to several preliminary gestures toward a more detailed reading.

In *Geschlecht I*, written roughly two years before *Geschlecht III*, Derrida alludes to his "interpretation to come" in *Geschlecht III* with the word "later." It is a question here of reading, in the strongest sense of that word, the a-sexual neutrality of *Dasein*—as Heidegger says, "*Dasein* is neither of the two sexes (*Geschlechtern*)"—as sexual nevertheless:

This clarification suggests that the sexless neutrality does not desexualize; on the contrary, its *ontological* negativity is not deployed with respect to *sexuality itself* (which it

12. Derrida and McDonald, "Choreographies," 76.
13. See below, p. 128.

would instead liberate), but with respect to the marks of difference, or more precisely to *sexual duality*. There would be no *Geschlechtslosigkeit* except with respect to the "two"; asexuality would be determined as such only to the degree that sexuality is immediately understood as binarity or sexual division. [. . .] If *Dasein* as such belongs to neither of the two sexes, that does not mean that as a being it is deprived of sex. On the contrary, here one must think of a pre-differential, or rather a pre-dual, sexuality—which does not necessarily mean unitary, homogeneous, and undifferentiated, as we shall be able to confirm later.[14]

In his reading of the 1928 Marburg lecture course, Derrida allows himself to read a more radical sexuality opened by this Heideggerian neutrality (with all the serious problems it entails), in particular because Heidegger specifies that this a-sexual neutrality is not the "indifference of an empty void (*die Indifferenz des leeren Nichtigen*) [. . .] but the original positivity (*ursprüngcliche Positivität*) and potency of the essence (*Mächtigkeit des Wesens*)."[15] If Heidegger himself never goes so far as to call this potent essence "sexual," this is no doubt for fear, as Derrida suggests, of "reintroduc[ing] the binary logic that anthropology and metaphysics always assign to the concept of sexuality."[16] This is what allows Derrida—in a way that is perhaps a bit "too violent," as he himself suspects—to make the link between the binary sexuality that Heidegger neutralizes and an impotent, neutral, and asexual negativity that would thus be "on the same side":

By returning to the originarity of *Dasein*, of this *Dasein* said to be sexually neutral, "original positivity" and "potency"

14. Derrida, *Psyche*, 2:14 (translation modified).
15. Martin Heidegger, *Metaphysical Foundations of Logic* (*GA* 26), trans. Michael Heim (Bloomington: Indiana University Press, 1984), 136.
16. Derrida, *Psyche*, 2:14.

can be recovered. In other words, despite appearances, the asexuality and neutrality that must first of all be subtracted from the binary sexual mark in the analytic of *Dasein* are in fact on the same side, on the side of *that* sexual difference— the binary one—to which one might have thought them simply opposed.[17]

In other words, a sexuality Derrida might have called "worthy of this name" would be rather on the side of the Heideggerian neutrality that, by neutralizing binary (a)sexual difference (that is, not a true difference but a dialectical identity of same and other), would ultimately be far less neutral and sterile than this binary difference, and would be on the way toward the other sexual difference that alone would merit the name.[18]

Now, *Geschlecht III* is precisely the text where Derrida pursues this sexuality opened by Heidegger's thought that would be more radical than the binary one. This time, the opening *takes place* in Heidegger's 1953 essay on Trakl, the very text that "magnetized" the entire *Geschlecht* series from the beginning. Even if this magnetization (*aimantation*) had always remained ambiguous—there are any number of signs of this in *Geschlecht I* and *II*—Derrida's rupture with Heidegger comes perhaps the most clearly exactly where we might have anticipated an absolute proximity (though does this ever exist between two lovers [*aimants*]?). Let us attempt to locate where the "later" evoked above is situated in order to see how Heideggerian sexual difference—"pre-dual, which does not necessarily mean unitary, homogeneous, and undifferentiated"—is not, despite appearances, altogether compatible with Derridean sexual difference.

17. Derrida, 2:15 (translation modified).
18. The discreet but absolutely crucial role of the idiom "worthy of the name" in Derrida has recently been thematized by Geoffrey Bennington in his *Scatter I: The Politics of Politics in Foucault, Heidegger, and Derrida* (New York: Fordham University Press, 2016), 238ff.

This moment can be situated very precisely. At the end of the Loyola typescript—whose thirty-three pages constitute, then, only the first part of *Geschlecht III*—Derrida seems to recall the "magnetization" he spoke of in *Geschlecht I*: "With some regret, I hasten toward the conclusion of this first part. What is said there of *Geschlecht* will have *magnetized* our entire reading."[19] Derrida is clearly referring to the first part of Heidegger's essay on Trakl, where a single sentence seems to gather the enigma of the text, as Derrida writes: "Here now is the formula that seems to me to carry the force and enigma of the text, the premises of which I attempted to indicate in the Marbug lecture course (1928): 'Not the twofold as such, but rather discord is the curse (*Nicht das Zwiefache als solches, sondern die Zwietracht ist der Fluch*).'"[20] Heidegger is committed to a *good* sexual difference that he opposes to the curse of the binary sexual war that has supposedly struck *Geschlecht* a second time. If the strike, blow, or imprint (*Schlag*) is what makes a *Geschlecht* a *Geschlecht* for Heidegger—who displaces the meaning of *Geschlecht* toward its etymological family (*gesleht* and *gislahti* are the collective forms of the Old German *slaht* for *Schlag*)—another strike seems to affect *Geschlecht* like an evil come upon it from the outside, and which ought to be avoided. This evil is nothing less than the sexual difference that makes sexual *difference* a *discord* that Heidegger would like to neutralize in a gentle and tender difference, a two-fold (*Zwiefalt*) whose duality remains that of a one-fold (*ein-fältig*), a "fold without fold," as Derrida translates *einfältigen Zwiefalt*.

Despite appearances, this Heideggerian sexual difference remains incompatible with Derrida's thought, which is suspi-

19. See below, p. 44 (my emphasis).
20. See below, p. 47. Derrida quotes Heidegger; Martin Heidegger, "Die Sprache im Gedicht: Eine Erörterung von Georg Trakls Gedicht," in *Unterwegs zur Sprache* (*GA* 12), ed. Friedrich-Wilhelm von Hermann (1959; Frankfurt am Main: Vittorio Klostermann, 1985), 46; Heidegger, "Language in the Poem: A Discussion of Georg Trakl's Poetic Work," in *On the Way to Language*, trans. Peter Hertz (New York: Harper & Row, 1971), 159–98.

cious of differential simplicity, or simplicity as such—a simplicity that, in Heidegger, will have always gathered difference into a unity whose value of gathering (*Versammlung*) remains problematic for Derrida and, what's more, unequal to the many "powerful deconstructive movements in Heidegger."[21] Going even further, Derrida suspects Heidegger of establishing a Platonic-Christian polarity between a good and bad strike that could only be, according to Derrida, two forms of the same, or of death: either the absolute presence of a place struck by a difference "without difference," the *einfältigen Zwiefalt*, or else the total absence of a non-place marked by disseminal errancy, that is, *Zwietracht*, unbridled dissension. For Derrida, it would be a question, rather, of going beyond, or stopping short of, this alternative and thinking the incessant compromise and negotiation between these two sides of death, which one must nevertheless try to survive—or, rather, "dream" of doing so:

> It must be, then, that relations be otherwise between place and non-place, gathering and divisibility (*différance*), that a sort of negotiation and compromise be continuously underway that requires us to rework the implicit logic that seems to guide Heidegger. To say that there is divisibility does not come down to saying that there is only divisibility or division either (this, too, would be death). Death lies in wait on both sides, on the side of the phantasm of the integrity of the proper place and the innocence of a sexual difference without war, and, on the opposite side, that of a radical impropriety or expropriation, or even a war of *Geschlecht* as sexual discord.[22]

*   *   *

21. See below, p. 82.

22. See below, p. 81–82. An argument of this kind can be found across Derrida's work; see in particular Jacques Derrida, *Of Grammatology*, trans. Gayatari Spivak (Baltimore: Johns Hopkins University Press, 2016). It is always a matter of thinking *différance between* the infinite and the finite, whose "problematic" and "conceptuality" must be "deconstructed," as Derrida writes.

In conclusion, another word on the 1984–85 seminar from which *Geschlecht III* is drawn. This was the first seminar Derrida gave at the EHESS, where he had recently been named *directeur d'études*. This seminar will be the first in a series of four seminars given under the general title *Philosophical Nationality and Nationalism* (1984–88). Even if *Geschlecht III* fits more closely within Derrida's tetralogy on Heidegger and *Geschlecht*, it is perhaps not unhelpful to reconstitute the thematic context of the seminar that forms the (never-saturated, let it be said) horizon of *Geschlecht III*. This is all the more worthwhile given that *Geschlecht II* is also drawn from the same seminar—the limit between the two texts indicated in the seminar by way of a marginal note in Derrida's hand to "stop here," that is, no doubt, stop the transcription of the seminar version of *Geschlecht II* into the version he gave as a lecture at Loyola, and which would later be published in *Psyche* without major revisions.

At the very beginning of *Geschlecht II*, Derrida alludes to the "invisible contexts" of this text and, by extension, of *Geschlecht III*:

> For lack of time, I can reconstitute neither the introductory article titled "*Geschlecht* I" (it discusses the motif of sexual difference in a lecture course more or less contemporary with *Sein und Zeit*), nor all the developments that form, in my seminar on "Philosophical Nationality and Nationalism," the contextual landscape of the reflections I will present to you today. Nevertheless, I will try to make the presentation of these few reflections, which are still preliminary, as intelligible and independent of all these invisible contexts as possible.[23]

Before delving into his long meditation on Heidegger and *Geschlecht*, Derrida attempts to situate his reading of Heidegger

23. Derrida, *Psyche*, 2:27–28.

within the thematic of his seminar, which deals with the essentially philosophical status of every nationalism and, conversely, the philosophical tendency that consists in supporting nationalism even (or *especially*) when a philosopher gives every appearance of being cosmopolitan—a tendency that can be quite extreme, going so far as to denounce one form of vulgar, biological-racial nationalism while surreptitiously affirming another form of nationalism. The national idiom, beyond the usual sense of the "linguistic" term—in particular the German idiom, or the *unsere Sprache* of Fichte or Heidegger (but also Adorno and Arendt)—will be, according to Derrida, the "ultimate recourse" of this more "profound" philosophical nationalism, which comes down not to affirming a simple linguistic nativity but rather to claiming a secret idiom, an "idiom of the idiom," which alone would provide "the sole true foundation of German nationality as German philosophy,"[24] a philosophical nationality that claims to be *the* (only) philosophy through which the universal of humanity is said and thought in German. Consequently, the name of this humanity—or, as Marx comments ironically, this "human nationality"—this *Geschlecht*, then, for Derrida "remains as problematic as that of the language in which the name is inscribed."[25]

In the seminar, Derrida begins to advance this hypothesis through a reading of Fichte, in particular his fundamental principle (*Grundsatz*) that would allow the German nation (or, strictly speaking, the German *Geschlecht*) to become what it must be destinally, according to the seventh of Fichte's

24. Jacques Derrida, *Philosophical Nationality and Nationalism I: The Ghost of the Other*, First Session, 1 (unpublished typescript). The first session of the 1984–85 seminar has been published in English, in a translation by Geoffrey Bennington, as "Onto-Theology National Humanism (Prolegomena to a Hypothesis)," *Oxford Literary Review* 14:1 (1992): 3–23. We quote this translation when appropriate; here, p. 15.

25. Derrida, *Psyche*, 2:31.

Addresses to the German Nation, in which Fichte addresses himself to (*Rede an*) the Germans:

> In the nation that to this day calls itself the people as such, or Germans, originality has in the modern age, at least until now burst forth in to the light of day, and the creative power of the new has shown itself; now, through a philosophy that has become clear to itself, a mirror is held up to this nation, a mirror in which it shall recognize with a clear concept that which, without distinct consciousness thereof, it has hitherto become through nature, and that to which it is called by nature (*wozu sie von derselben bestimmt ist*). And to this nation a proposal is made, according to this clear concept and with deliberate and free art: to make itself wholly and completely into what it ought to be, to renew the covenant and to close the circle. The principle according to which it must close the circle we have laid before the nation. Whatever believes in spirituality and in the freedom of this spirituality, whatever desires the eternal progress of this spirituality through freedom—wherever it may be born and whichever language it may speak—is of our *Geschlecht*, it belongs to us and will join with us.[26]

The difficulty of this passage revolves around a problem of translation: how to translate "*Geschlecht*"? Or, a far more serious problem, *must* we or *can* we translate it according to Fichte? Is it in fact an irreducibly German word that says something essential about a humanity we should therefore refer to as *Menschengeschlecht*, for fear of not being able to access that very thing this word can name only in German?

26. Johann Gottlieb Fichte, *Addresses to the German Nation*, ed. and trans. Gregory Moore (Cambridge: Cambridge University Press, 2009), 97. We have modified the published translation here in accordance with Derrida's own choices when translating Fichte into French. For reasons that are perhaps already clear, we will not attempt to translate "*Geschlecht*."

At first glance, Fichte's gesture may seem innocent of any nationalism of a biological, racial, linguistic, ethnic, or even politico-state *type*. As Derrida suggests,

> This *Geschlecht* is, then, not determined by birth, native soil, or race; it has nothing natural or even linguistic about it, at least not in the usual sense of this term [. . .]. The sole analytic and unimpeachable determination of *Geschlecht* in this context is the "we," the belonging to the "we" to whom we are speaking at this moment, at the moment that Fichte addresses himself to this supposed but still to be constituted community, a community that, strictly speaking, is neither political, nor racial, nor linguistic, but that can receive his allocution, his address, or his apostrophe (*Rede an . . .*), and can think with him, can say "we" in any language and from any birthplace whatever.[27]

Given the highly undetermined status of this "we" and of "our *Geschlecht*"—an "infinite 'we,' a 'we' that announces itself to itself from the infinity of a *telos* of freedom and spirituality [. . .], a 'we' of spiritual freedom engaged in its infinite progress"[28]—one could, perhaps, forgive the French translator, Samuel Jankélévitch, who was in fact a Russian Jewish emigrant translating Fichte in French "during or shortly after the war," for his decision to retreat when faced with the risk—a political risk for him, as well—of translating the word "*Geschlecht*" (especially as "race") and for quite simply omitting the word. In doing so, however, French readers no longer notice what Derrida calls an "essential *Deutschheit*"[29] in Fichte's text, no doubt picking up on the title of Fichte's

27. Derrida, *Psyche*, 2:29 (translation modified).
28. Derrida, 2:29.
29. Derrida, 2:29.

seventh discourse, "A yet deeper understanding of the originality and Germanity (*Deutschheit*) of a people":

> How is "*Geschlecht*" to be translated under these conditions? Fichte uses a word that *already* has a vast wealth of semantic determinations in his language, and he speaks *German*. Say as he might: anyone, in whatever language he speaks, "*ist unsers Geschlechts*," he says it in German, and this *Geschlecht* is an essential *Deutschheit*. Even if the word *Geschlecht* acquires a rigorous content only from out of the "we" instituted by that very address, it also includes connotations indispensable to the minimal intelligibility of the discourse, and these connotations belong irreducibly to German, to a German more essential than all the phenomena of empirical Germanity but to something German nevertheless (*mais à de l'allemand*). [. . .] How are we to translate?[30]

In other words, how are we to translate into a Romance language something that can be said only in German, a secret German, as it were, that some native Germans have never heard of, to be sure, but a German *nevertheless*, the Germanity of which will transgress geo-politico-physical borders, yet without ever being confused with non-German. This is where Fichte's apparently inclusive and hospitable gesture joins up with an imperialist, "annexationist and expansionist" tendency, as Derrida reminds us:

> The essence of German is not to be confused with empirical factuality, with empirical belonging to the factual German nation, any more than empirical non-belonging to that German nation excludes non-Germans from participation in some originary Germanity. [. . .] Whence this paradoxical consequence, which one can consider either as an expansion of generosity, or as the imperialist expansionism of

30. Derrida, 2:29.

a people sure of itself, and dominant: whoever shares in this originary philosophy—of originarity, of life, of creative freedom—is German, even if they apparently belong to another people.[31]

Conversely, whoever refuses to believe and to want—following Fichte's *Grundsatz*—spiritual freedom to be infinitely perfected does not merely have a difference of opinion, that person is radically excluded from a Germanity that will be conflated with the creative force of the new and the originary life of German philosophy, which, in turn, is not merely one philosophy among others, but the best and most living philosophy, which must be protected and purified from harmful internal forces. Here is how Fichte follows the articulation of his fundamental principle:

> Those who believe in stagnation, retrogression and circularity, and even set a dead nature at the helm of world government—wherever they were born and whichever language they speak—are non-Germans (*undeutsch*) and strangers to us, and *it is to be wished that the sooner they completely cut themselves off from us the better.* [. . .] What this philosophy that rightly calls itself German philosophy actually wants, and wherein it is opposed with earnestness and unrelenting rigor to every foreign philosophy with a belief in death, is finally given voice, and he that hath ears to hear, let him hear. And it is given voice not so that those who are dead shall understand it, which is impossible, *but so that it shall become more difficult for them to distort its words* (*die Worte verdrehen*).[32]

This would be the "ultimate recourse" of Fichtean nationalism: what is German must be *guarded* and immunized against

---

31. Derrida, "Onto-Theology," 12–13 (translation modified).
32. Fichte, *Addresses to the German Nation*, 97.

any and all contamination, especially if it comes from the inside by way of false Germans who do not speak true German, and who must therefore be gotten rid of as quickly as possible for fear that these dead or ghostly foreigners corrupt the language.[33]

We find the same argument in the fourth of Fichte's *Addresses*, where the introduction of the foreign language into German, especially words of a "Roman origin," risks "clearly downgrad[ing] their moral way of thinking" (*ihre sittliche Denkart offenbar herunterstimmen*).[34] The first word Fichte cites in this context is the word "*Humanität*," which for a German remains a "completely empty noise" (*ein völlig leerer Schall*) on account of its Romano-Latin origin.[35] But, says Fichte, "if instead of the word '*Humanität*,' we had said '*Menschlichkeit*' [but also *Menschheit* or *Menschengeschlecht*] to a German, he would have understood us without any further historical explanation."[36] For Fichte, this is because the German word "*Menschlichkeit*" remains a sensuous concept (*ein sinnlicher Begriff*) immediately linked to a concrete intuition—animated in fact by the spiritual breath of the German language, "which is born out of the common and uninterrupted life of people whose intuitions that language continues to espouse"—whereas *humanitas* was already, in a dead language, "cut off from its

33. This "return of the phantom" in Fichte's German no doubt inspired the title of the 1984–85 seminar, *The Ghost of the Other*; see the handwritten note in the margin: "Nationalism and haunting, return of the ghost. Between life and death, nationalism has its proper place in the experience of haunting. No nationalism without some ghost" (Derrida, "Onto-Theology," 15). On this point, see also what Derrida will say in *Geschlecht III* (below, pp. 54–55) about the "value of *Geist*, phantom, ghost" that Heidegger does not put to work but nevertheless seems in Derrida's view to "impose itself and be motivated by the whole context"; see also Jacques Derrida, *Of Spirit: Heidegger and the Question*, trans. Geoffrey Bennington and Rachel Bowlby (Chicago: University of Chicago Press, 1991).

34. Fichte, *Addresses to the German Nation*, 52–53.

35. Fichte, 55.

36. Fichte, 55.

living roots," an abstract, lifeless, and ghostly symbol (*Sinn-bild*) of a supersensuous Roman and foreign idea that can cunningly invade German in such an artificial way that it denatures its essential *Deutschheit* and its *Geschlecht*: once again, the "return of the phantom" and the nefarious ghostly evil that *works on* the idiom and every nationalism.

Starting from this reading of Fichte, Derrida identifies what he calls the "paradoxical but regular association of nationalism with cosmopolitanism and with humanism."[37] Far from being an empirical particularity, nationalism would consist in electing one nation that claims to represent or incarnate, better than any other and most especially through its idiom, the essence of humanity in an exemplary way, to the point of expanding and essentializing this nationality to humanity itself, such that access to humanity remains the exclusive privilege of *this* nationality—and *its idiom*—which therefore claims to be essentially cosmopolitico-universal and "philosophical by that very fact":

> This concerns the structure of national consciousness, feeling and demand which means that a nation posits itself not only a bearer of a philosophy but of an exemplary philosophy, i.e., one that is both particular and potentially universal—and which is philosophical by that very fact. [. . .] Fichte's famous *Addresses to the German Nation* [. . .] wants to be both nationalistic, patriotic and cosmopolitan, universalistic. It essentializes Germanity to the point of making it an entity bearing the universal and the philosophical as such.[38]

This means that, despite its innocent appearance, Fichtean nationalism remains at the very least equivocal with respect to a "reappropriation into a Nazi heritage"; as Derrida reminds us,

37. Derrida, *Psyche*, 2:24.
38. Derrida, "Onto-Theology," 10–11.

"It is in the name of a philosophy of life (even if it is spiritual life) that it sets itself apart from naturalizing biologism."[39] This equivocality, which Derrida characterizes as "extreme and threatening, worrying, murky," would be "preparatory [. . .] of the most sinister and unavoidable modernity," that of Nazism, to be sure, but also that of "today and tomorrow."[40]

Nevertheless, it is necessary to make clear that for Derrida the "sequence of German national-philosophism" would not merely be one example of nationalism among others. Although he looks at other forms of nationalism during the first half of the seminar before getting to Heidegger—other nationalities of nationalism, as it were (like those of Hume, Quinet, Michelet, Tocqueville, and Adonis)—Derrida pursues first and foremost a reading of several German thinkers (Kant, Hegel, Marx, Grün, Adorno, Wittgenstein, Arendt), following the motif of a nationalism smuggled into their works (with the exception of Marx), a very implicit and occasionally unavowed nationalism (especially in the case of Adorno and Arendt), precisely when they make every effort to critique the most vulgar type of nationalism, yet without dispelling the sinisterly ironic and nationalist equivocality their critique relies on without their realizing it. The German idiom will always be, even in *its* silence, the force that gathers even the most opposite ends of the philosophico-political spectrum together around a language believed to have an "elective affinity" (Adorno's *Wahlverwandtschaft*) and an exclusive privilege vis-à-vis philosophy, humanity, and the universal.[41] And the word through which this philosophical nation claims uniquely to say humanity and the universal—"*Geschlecht*," precisely—

39. Derrida, 16.
40. Derrida, 16.
41. Theodor W. Adorno, "On the Question: 'What Is German?,'" trans. Thomas Y. Levin, *New German Critique* 36 (Autumn 1985): 121–31; quoted by Derrida in *Philosophical Nationality and Nationalism I*, Third Session, 7 (unpublished typescript).

becomes exemplary for Derrida with respect to the national-humanist problematic.

In this context, Heidegger—and Heidegger's German, his German that is Old and High, secret, idiomatico-poetic, which is to say more or less untranslatable and even silent, including his idiomatic appropriation of Trakl's "Ein [*One*] *Geschlecht*," which resonates perhaps with the *Geschlecht* or the "we" of Fichte—will play a central role according to Derrida when it comes to thinking nationalism today, "this enigmatic event [. . .] that passes by way of this thing that is so difficult to think that we call 'Germany' and 'German philosophy.' "[42] On this point, we refer the reader of *Geschlecht III* to a Heidegger letter dated December 15, 1945—which Derrida quotes several times in the 1984–85 seminar and in *Geschlecht II*—addressed to Constantin von Dietze, the president of the Purification Committee meant to denazify Freiburg University:

> I believed that Hitler, after having assumed the responsibility of the entire people (*Volk*), would outgrow the party and its doctrine, and that everything would come together on the basis of a renewal and a gathering unto a Western responsibility. This belief was an error I recognized after the events of June 30, 1934. In 1933/34, it brought me to an intermediate position, in that I affirmed the national and the social (but not the nationalistic) and rejected the intellectual and metaphysical foundation laid by the biologism of the party doctrine, because the social and the national, as I saw it, were not essentially tied to the biologico-racial worldview doctrine.[43]

According to Derrida, one finds in this letter "the same terms" as in Fichte's nationalism, which also wants to distinguish

---

42. Derrida, *Philosophical Nationality and Nationalism I*, Second Session, 3 (unpublished typescript).

43. Martin Heidegger, *Reden und anderen Zeugnisse eines Lebensweges* (*GA* 16), ed. Hermann Heidegger (Frankfurt am Main: Vittorio Klostermann, 2000), 489; quoted in Derrida, *Psyche*, 2:32.

itself—without totally managing to do so, according to Derrida—from any biological or racial nationalism. In a way, all the weight of Derrida's argument in *Geschlecht III* bears on the denunciation of a profound, subtle, and troubling nationalism-humanism in Heidegger's thought—a thought that remains at the very least ambiguous with respect to the Nazism and humanism from which it seeks to distance itself. This would be the more strictly political side—or pole—of *Geschlecht III*, what Derrida calls "another, perhaps less visible, dimension of the *same* [political] drama" in Heidegger that had already become in France in 1985, before the irruption of the Victor Farías phenomenon, a "bit too academic" in his eyes.[44] It goes without saying that today, after the publication of the *Black Notebooks* (*Schwarze Hefte*) and their burning political content, Derrida's patience and prudence concerning rather polemical themes in Heidegger—the "*One* Geschlecht" of "our language" that must, as the mission of its destiny and "in view of a responsibility of the West," save the earth from the corrupt and decomposing *Geschlecht* (*das verwesende Geschlecht*)—as well as the rigor of deconstructive reading can only appreciably enrich the debate, to the point of upending its premises. The same could be said for contemporary reflection on the quite frightening resurgence of nationalism today.

Rodrigo Therezo
Freiburg-im-Breisgau, July 2017

44. Derrida, *Psyche*, 2:32.

Jacques Derrida did not complete *Geschlecht III* during his lifetime. The present volume thus edits two unpublished texts that, together, represent Derrida's most advanced work on this project, a meticulous reading of Heidegger's essay on Georg Trakl, "Language in the Poem," from *On the Way to Language*.

The first of these texts is a thirty-three-page typescript that Derrida distributed to some of the participants of a conference held at Loyola University in Chicago, March 22–23, 1985; it was at this same conference that Derrida also presented the previous installment in his *Geschlecht* series, "Heidegger's Hand (*Geschlecht II*)." For three decades, this unpublished "Loyola typescript" was all of *Geschlecht III* that was believed to exist.

As it turns out, however, the Loyola typescript is only a first, "unfinished and incomplete" part of the entirety of *Geschlecht III*. The second part is drawn from Derrida's 1984–85 seminar titled *The Ghost of the Other*, the first of four seminars he gave under the general title *Philosophical Nationality and Nationalism* at the École des Hautes Études en Sciences Sociales (EHESS) in Paris. Our edition picks up the text of the *Ghost of the Other* seminar at the place where the Loyola typescript stops—this latter text being, according to Derrida, a "transcription" of thirty or so pages of the seminar; the Loyola typescript corresponds to the portion of the seminar that runs from page 12 of the Seventh Session to the end of the Eighth Session. What follows the text of the Loyola typescript in this edition are the five sessions of the seminar that, according to Derrida, "remained to be transcribed" when he distributed the Loyola typescript in Chicago, just two days after having concluded the *Ghost of the Other* seminar in Paris.

This edition reproduces the complete text of *Geschlecht III*, which is thus comprised of the Loyola typescript plus the five last sessions (the Ninth Session to the Thirteenth Session) of the 1984–85 seminar.

*   *   *

Our editorial work is guided by the conventions established for the publication of Jacques Derrida's seminars. Our interventions in the typescripts (the "Loyola" typescript and that of the seminar) are as minimal as possible. We have preserved Derrida's punctuation (even in the case of very long sentences), with just a few exceptions where we restore, for example, an unclosed parenthesis or a necessary comma. We have also corrected the occasional typo and added words or punctuation marks in angled brackets (<word>) to fill in certain gaps in the typescript. When the syntax is incomplete, we have indicated this fact in a footnote ("As such in the typescript").

As for bibliographic references, *Geschlecht III* is a text that quotes very frequently, but from a limited number of texts. The aforementioned Heidegger essay provides the vast majority of the quotations. We restore the quotation marks each time Derrida omits them (which happens frequently), when it is clear that it is a question of a direct quotation and not paraphrase. The reader will note that when Derrida translates Heidegger himself, he does not hesitate to propose two or three possible translations of the same word or phrase, which, in our view, does not constitute a paraphrase but indeed a quotation, which is thus indicated as such.

As for the editions consulted by Derrida, we of course remain faithful to those texts. However, for the Heidegger works quoted in German, we have adopted the pagination of the *Gesamtausgabe* (*GA*) volumes. For the Trakl poems quoted by Derrida, we provide the page in "Die Sprache im Gedicht" where Heidegger refers to them; when there are lines or poems not quoted by Heidegger, we provide references to recent German editions of Trakl. At two points in the typescript of the seminar, Derrida does not transcribe the text of a long quotation but simply indicates the pages to be read; in these two cases, we had recourse to his personal library held at Princeton University in order to identify the passages in question in his books, where he indicated them with brackets.

As to the preparation of the first part of the text, the Loyola typescript served as the base text, but we have also indicated particularly important or illuminating variations in the seminar version. We reproduce these passages in footnotes, marked with the abbreviation S.V. (Seminar Version).

During our archival research at the Institut Mémoire de l'Édition Contemporaine (IMEC) in France, we also discovered a third, previously unknown version of the first fifteen pages of the text of *Geschlecht III*, where Derrida begins the text by addressing "the reader." This is no doubt a preliminary version—likely drafted between the seminar and the Loyola typescript—that Derrida was preparing for a future publication but evidently abandoned early on. Nevertheless, we found interesting passages there that noticeably enrich the text, particularly concerning the concept of reading. As with the variations issuing from the seminar, we reproduce these passages in footnotes with the abbreviation I.V. (Intermediate Version).

Nearly the entirety of the texts used was typewritten. There are, however, four handwritten pages in the seminar text that had to be deciphered. The seminar also contains several notes in Derrida's hand, written in the margin in the typescript. We have transcribed these additions whenever possible and provided them in the footnoes.

Unless otherwise indicated, all notes are those of the editors.

Editors' Note [xxxiii]

*　　*　　*

We would like to thank David Farrell Krell for his singular and unwavering interest in *Geschlecht III* over many years; we also thank Jean-Luc Nancy and Avital Ronell for their enthusiasm for this project; above all, we wish to express our deep gratitude to Marguerite Derrida, Jean Derrida, and Pierre Alferi for their support and confidence.

Geoffrey Bennington
Katie Chenoweth
Rodrigo Therezo

GESCHLECHT III

Our progression will be slow, irregular in its rhythm, following an itinerary that no linear representation could describe.[1]
Isn't calling it a "progression" already overstating an approach
that might give the feeling, annoying to some, that it lets itself be paralyzed by its very insistence: we are not moving
forward, we are turning in circles, we are backtracking. Apparently without gaining any ground, without occupying any
position, renouncing every concern for discursive strategy.
And then, all of a sudden, abrupt jumps, leaps, and zigzags,
decided each time; and we do not know whether these singular ruptures have been carefully calculated or if they have
surprised the discourse, come to it as the event of the other,
decided from the other.

It is first of all Heidegger's manner that we are describing in
this way; others would have said his "style," his style of thinking or writing. I prefer to say his "manner" for reasons that are
clearer now. The question of rhythm becomes complicated
here. Heidegger indeed poses this question, as we shall see,
and it is tempting more than it is legitimate to fold back onto

---

1. Intermediate Version (I.V.): "It would be best to warn the reader: from
this point on, our progression will be as slow as possible, irregular in its
rhythm, following an itinerary that no linear representation would be able,
I believe, to describe."

his writing what he interprets as the essence of poetic rhythm, beyond its "metaphysico-aesthetic representation."[2]

In order to "read" Heidegger, to follow him without barbaric violence, without unjust or unfaithful violence, in order to hear him without walling oneself up in the deaf passivity of commentary, must we not simultaneously regulate our steps with his and deregulate them? Must we not disturb their cadence, slow down when he goes too fast, interrupt a jump, suspend its gesture or, instead, leap all at once toward a given detour, at the turning point of a lengthy procedure?[3]

2. Martin Heidegger, "Die Sprache im Gedicht: Eine Erörterung von Georg Trakls Gedicht," in *Unterwegs zur Sprache* (*GA* 12), ed. Friedrich-Wilhelm von Hermann (1959; Frankfurt am Main: Vittorio Klostermann, 1985), 34.

The French translations of this essay found in *Geschlecht III*—that is, the published French translation by Jean Beaufret and Wolfgang Brokmeier, to which Derrida has recourse throughout, but also his own frequent retranslations of Heidegger into French—differ significantly from the published English translation of "Language in the Poem." While the English translator Peter Hertz adopts a rather free style of translation, Derrida tends to translate in a more literal way that tracks Heidegger's German closely. We have thus opted to retranslate into English the numerous quoted passages from Heidegger's essay that appear in *Geschlecht III* in a similarly literal fashion, with an eye to the choices Derrida makes when translating Heidegger into French. On occasion, when Derrida makes a special point of quoting and commenting on Beaufret and Brokmeier's translation, we have translated this version into English in the body of the text and provided a more literal translation of Heidegger's German in a footnote. For reference, we provide the German pagination of Heidegger's essay throughout. The reader may also wish to consult Hertz's English translation: Martin Heidegger, "Language in the Poem: A Discussion of Georg Trakl's Poetic Work," in *On the Way to Language*, trans. Peter Hertz (New York: Harper & Row, 1971), 159–98. (—Trans.)

3. I.V.: "*Captatio benevolentiae*: may the reader not lose patience. Heidegger's text is already very difficult (secret) in its original language; we do not say it enough. It is barely readable in the best translations, at least in those places where the decisive resources of his discourse or of his demonstrations retain an untranslatable tie to the German language.* What to say, then, of the difficulty of the position in which whoever writes after Heidegger, according to him and "on" him, must struggle, between multiple languages and multiple imperatives (to debate, respond, etc.)? These con-

The first essay I attempted under the title "*Geschlecht*" was largely concerned with a text from 1928 and mentioned this date at the outset.⁴ It announced an approach to this essay from 1953. The very neutral mention of these two dates, 1928 for the Marburg lecture course, 1953 for "Die Sprache im Gedicht," does not suggest some regular evolution in what one would call "the thought-of-Heidegger."⁵ We do not have at

<hr />

siderations are not merely preliminary. As we will confirm, they already go straight to what is most at stake in the debate." [*Derrida's note: I will nevertheless have recourse, very frequently, to the invaluable translation published by Jean Beaufret and Wolfgang Brokmeier in the *NRF* (January–February 1958), now collected in Martin Heidegger, *Acheminement vers la parole* [*On the Way to Language*] (Paris: Gallimard, 1976), p. 39 sq. With each step the risk of thinking remains intimately engaged in language, the idiom, and translation. I salute the audacious adventure that such a translation, in its very discretion, has constituted. Our debt is here toward a gift that gives far more than what one calls a "French version." Every time I will be obliged to stray from this translation, it will be without the slightest intention of evaluating it, still less of amending it. It will be necessary, rather, for us to multiply the drafts, to harass the German word and analyze it according to multiple waves of touches, caresses, or blows. A translation, in the usual sense of what is published under this name, cannot allow itself to do this. But it is on the contrary our duty to do it every time the calculus of the word-for-word, one word for another, in other words the conventional ideal of translation, will be put to the challenge. It would, moreover, be legitimate—apparently trivial but in truth essential—to take this text on Trakl as a situation (*Erörterung*) of what we call translating. At the heart of this situation, of this site (*Ort*), is *Geschlecht*, the word or the mark. For it is the composition and decomposition of this mark, Heidegger's work in his language, his manual and artisanal writing, his *Hand-Werk*, that the existing translations (French and, I imagine, English) inevitably tend to erase.]

4. Jacques Derrida, "*Geschlecht* I: Sexual Difference, Ontological Difference," in *Psyche: Inventions of the Other*, vol. 2, ed. Peggy Kamuf and Elizabeth Rottenberg (Stanford, CA: Stanford University Press, 2008), 7–26.

5. Martin Heidegger, *Metaphysische Anfangsgründe der Logik im Ausgang von Leibniz* (*GA* 26), ed. Klaus Held (1978; Frankfurt am Main: Vittorio Klostermann, 2007); *The Metaphysical Foundations of Logic*, trans. Michael Heim (Bloomington: Indiana University Press, 1984).

I.V.: "Two dates are also two signatures. To date is to sign a delivery from a given place, on a given date. Speaking precisely of the place, of the site (*Ort*) and situation (*Erörterung*), Heidegger does not speak of *Geschlecht*

our disposal, by means of these simple dates, reference points from which to measure, put into perspective, assure ourselves of a bird's-eye view, stake out a course. Nevertheless, if I mark these two stations or these two places, it is because I do mean to clarify some *relation*. As with each of the words on which we will have to take a risk, in French as well as in German (*Bezug, Zug, ziehen, entziehen,* etc.), the word "*relation*" [*rapport*] appears to be very loaded. To anticipate abruptly, we

---

when he writes on the trail of Trakl, on the road (*unterwegs*) with the poet of *Unterwegs* as he spoke of *Geschlecht* in a course a quarter of a century earlier. Just because a course and the accompanying of a poetic speech can say the same thing—and this is perhaps the case here—they would not be able to say it identically, especially twenty-five years apart (and these twenty-five years are also something other than an interval in a movement forward . . .). In 1928 and in 1953—this is my question—is Heidegger saying the same thing? The same thing said otherwise? And what else, then? It happens—let us say this again before even beginning—that if these two texts say differently the same thing, if they imprint differently the same thing, a strike (*Schlag*) according to an imprinting (*Wortprägung*), a blow, an import right on *Geschlecht*, it is because they belong perhaps to the same *Geschlecht*. But what does *Geschlecht* mean? Sex, race, species, genus, family, stock, etc. And first 'type,' a word that refers back to *tuptein*, to strike: 'Our language,' Heidegger says, 'calls *Geschlecht* the human essence (*Menschenwesen*) in which this strike has imprinted itself and which through this strike is separated, specified (*verschlagene*)' ("*Die Sprache im Gedicht,*" p. 45). *Verschlagene* in its usual sense means 'separated.' Here the separation is specifying, it is what gives the blow, the imprint marking the human kind, the human species. Now, within, as it were, this general or generic strike, which applies both to the human type and to familial stocks or kinships, another strike has imprinted its type, a supplementary strike, as it were, the duality of the sexes. It is indeed a question of a supplementary strike or typography that comes once again (*wiederum*) to imprint its mark: '*dies alles wiederum geprägt in das Zwiefache der Geschlechter*' (ibid., p. 46). In the Marburg course, the word *Geschlecht* was always very narrowly determined, by the context, and assigned not only to sexuality but to sexuality divided in two. Here, division happens to *Geschlecht*. We will be obliged to think, in tandem with the poet, a certain unity, or rather the 'one' of *Geschlecht* that is not yet 'either unisexuality (*Eingeschlechtlichkeit*), nor undifferentiation or sexual equivalence (*Gleichgeschlechtlichkeit*)' (ibid., p. 74). We find again the *Mannigfaltigkeit* and the *Streuung* of Marburg."

[4] *Geschlecht III*

see being announced that, in the question of *Geschlecht* and of "*Geschlecht*"—of the thing, word, or mark (and before the question, which is then no longer the most general term, there is the mark), of a thing, word, or mark that never again rest in their essence of thing or word—there is not only a provocation to think relation as reference, as a relation of word to thing, nor only the sexual relation (*Geschlechtsverkehr*), but also a relation of the one to the two in which the fold of reference as difference precedes a certain duality or situates itself between two forms of the two, the second form coming to remark the first so as to affect it with dissension. How, then, could we easily receive this word "relation"? To relate two texts, two places, two dates: what could this really mean? Why might it matter?

No doubt I will try to relate, modestly, several readings of *Geschlecht*, of "*Geschlecht*" to one another, leaving behind the outline of so many other possible itineraries. But the word "reading" *also* lets itself be affected by this re-situation of *Geschlecht*. We cannot, therefore, rely on any easy assurance when it comes to this word. I will no doubt try in turn to "read" Heidegger's "reading" of certain poems by Trakl. No doubt have I already, quite implicitly and banking on conventions and complicities, overburdened this word "reading" with what a number of works, French ones in particular, have succeeded in determining or transforming over the past twenty years. I will no doubt attempt, on the basis of this "reading," to transpose, generalize, or problematize what a "type" of Heideggerian reading might be. A type, which is also to say a "stroke" [*coup*] of reading: not a model, procedure, or method but a *typed* [*typé*] pathway. The *tuptein* of the *tupos* does not primarily refer here to some *tympan* I may have described long ago, or to Lacoue-Labarthe's remarkable *Typographies* but, precisely, to what links the *tupos* to the *Schlag*, and thus to *Geschlecht* in Heidegger's text.[6] Besides the value of impression, blow,

6. Jacques Derrida, "Tympan," in *Margins of Philosophy*, trans. Alan Bass (Chicago: University of Chicago Press, 1982), ix-xxix; Philippe Lacoue-Labarthe,

strike, or inscription, our attention is here called back to that of regularity, iterability, thus of re-impression in the re-mark. A type is not only the moment or place of the strike, it already introduces the generality of the genus [*genre*], it remains or produces, it reproduces the same for a series of singularities

---

Typography, ed. Christopher Fynsk (Stanford, CA: Stanford University Press, 1998).

Derrida's note: *Typographies I* is the subtitle of the book titled *Le Sujet de la philosophie* (Paris: Flammarion, 1979) and "Typography" the title of an essay published in *Mimesis des articulations* (Paris: Flammarion, 1975). This last essay quotes (p. 181 sq.) and analyzes the allusion that Heidegger makes to the *tupos* in *Zur Seinsfrage* after a reference to the *Theaetatus* (192–194b): "*Das Her-vor-bringende ist von Platon bisweilen als das Prägende (typos) gedacht* (That which brings to the fore is on occasion thought by Plato as that which imprints (*tupos*))." (German text in "Zur Seinsfrage," in *Wegmarken* [*GA 9*] [Frankfurt am Main, Vittorio Klostermann, 1976], 395; "On the Question of Being," trans. William McNeill, in *Pathmarks*, ed. William McNeill [Cambridge: Cambridge University Press, 1998], 299.) Heidegger addresses Jünger: "You too think the relation of form to that which it "forms" as a relation of stamping and imprinting (*als das Verhältnis von Stempel und Prägung*). However, you understand imprinting (*Prägen*) in the modern sense as a conferring of meaning upon that which is meaningless. Form (*Gestalt*) is 'the source that gives meaning' (*Sinngebung*) (The Worker, 148)." (Ibid.) What is thus determined as "modernity" is not the figure of the *imprint* in itself, but an interpretation of *Prägen* as giving meaning. This modernity is also that of subjectity, of humanity as subjectity, this humanity, this human type that would be considered as the giving source of meaning. We see the expression "*Menschenschlag*" appear in this context: "In another respect, however, the metaphysical representation that occurs in *The Worker* is distinct from Platonic and even from modern representation, that of Nietzsche excepted. The source that gives meaning, the power that is present in advance and thus leaves its imprint on everything (*die im vorhinein präsente und so alles prägende Macht*), is the form as the form of a particular *kind of human* (*Menschentums*): "the form of the Worker." The form resides in the essential configuration of a kind of human that, as subjectum, underlies all beings. It is not the individual human being as an "I," the subjectity of an *ego*, but the preformed and form-like presence of a particular cast (*tupos*) of human (*die vorgeformte gestalthafte Praesenz eines Menschenschlages*) that constitutes the most extreme subjectity, which comes to the fore in the consummation of modern metaphysics and is presented through its thinking" (396).

[6] *Geschlecht III*

that thus fall under the *same type*—which can only be typical on the condition of the same.

A typology is implied in the set of classical questions: what law gives its regularity to Heidegger's typical gestures? Because a signature is of a type. How does Heidegger read? How does he write? What are the movements by which we recognize his mark? In particular in the treatment or handling (*Handlung*), the manner not of treating (he would say) but of listening to a "poetic" text and calling attention to this rather than that? Interpretation? Hermeneutics? Poetics? Philology? Literary criticism or theory? Clearly not: Heidegger's typical gesture does not present itself under any of these headings, and it is necessary at least to begin by taking this self-presentation into account, whatever conclusions one may draw from it in the end. Is it then a matter of a philosophical reading? Not that either, and not only because this is not a "reading" but because philosophy is here situated rather then situating. *Thought* here is not reducible to philosophy; on the contrary, it demarcates itself from philosophy in an essential way without becoming simply poetic. We will return later to the "parallelism" and distance between *Denken* and *Dichten*.⁷

What can the limits of this *type* of thought be, then, which presents itself first of all as a thought of the type? A limit is not always negative, as Heidegger often recalls.⁸ It makes possible and it gives rise [*donne lieu*]. A place [*lieu*] takes place only within limits. The question, then, is that of Heidegger's place, some may say. Perhaps, but in saying that we are mimicking,

7. Martin Heidegger, "Das Wesen der Sprache," in *Unterwegs*, 85.

8. Seminar Version (S.V.): "*All* these questions likely have some legitimacy. I hope that those who are interested in them (a group from which I do not exclude myself) will recognize at least a concern for them throughout what I am about to attempt now. The stakes of Heidegger's thought today seem such that the elaboration of questions like these could not be useless. But for this very reason, it is also urgent to situate what the classical forms of these questions presuppose, neglect, or dissimulate. I will take just two examples, to begin, as a preliminary indication."

reproducing, folding back on Heidegger the gesture of situation (*Erörterung*) that he makes in relation to Trakl. We must then envision, in order to prepare ourselves for it, still something other than a situation of Heidegger. This would be the condition for having access to the presuppositions that may uphold Heidegger's particular situation of Trakl's *Gedicht*, and, already, to the general determination of the essence of place (*Ortschaft*) that is at work here. Before we even reach (if this is possible) these presuppositions, let us at least take stock of this fact.[9] All the classical questions, or even the objections directed at Heidegger from the point of view of philology, poetics, hermeneutics, literary science, even philosophy presuppose, even more critically than the possibility of an essence of place, the simple existence of a place; and in particular for an oeuvre or corpus, that singular place that a textual locality is. Heidegger proposes from the outset to rethink place, locality, site, situation: so many translations that are already inadequate since they lose the unity of co-belonging among *Ort, Ortschaft, Erörterung*. This last word, which in everyday language is more or less synonymous with discussion, debate, etc., is here called back, from the opening lines, toward the situation of the place, the gesture that seeks to indicate the proper site. All of this thus no longer falls under the classical disciplines and problematics we just mentioned: philology, poetics, literary criticism, philosophico-literary theory, hermeneutics or philosophy, etc. It does not even belong to a fundamental theory or axiomatics of reading.[10] The motifs

9. What follows will be the first of the "two examples" Derrida mentions in the seminar (see previous note). He will neglect, however, to provide a second example, which will appear only in the intermediate version of the text (see next note).

10. I.V.: "Second example, second preliminary indication: the concept of reading. Let us recall this trivial fact. No matter how it is further developed, the concept of reading is never constructed without that of a writing, that which gives reading or itself to read, or which engages (itself) at the heart of reading itself. No writing without the mark, trace, imprint, inscription, incision, blow. Now, we will come to this, this pathway toward a locality

of foundation or axiom are themselves also delimited and situated along the way in *Der Satz vom Grund*.[11] They cannot constitute a final recourse for thought. We should at least recognize that the juridico-epistemological theme of the "final

---

passes necessarily by way of a thinking of *Geschlecht* as a thinking of the blow (*Schlag*) and of repetition, of the redoubled blow, of the "good" and "bad" blow. Let us not go further than this signal for the moment. If the question "after" [*d'après*] the place and concerning *Geschlecht* (which does not only mean, does not yet mean "sexuality"), as a question of the blow, mark, strike, imprint, can no longer be limited to one example among others, among all those that fall under a hypothetical general theory of reading and writing, it could not be submitted to all the transcendental, epistemological, or methodological protocols of such a "theory." Attempting to accompany Heidegger in this path of thought with the greatest possible patience and caution—and caution, Heidegger's caution, does not exclude risk, quite the contrary, or engagement: we risk or wager (*wagen*) enough, already, he says, from the first lines, if we content ourselves with these steps on the threshold—but following him also with the least possible reservation, this does not commit the approach to the genre of docile or passive commentary. Rather, this requires that without being overly hasty [*se presser*] to object, we press [*on presse*] the text to be read with questions and, as much as possible, preferably, with questions that seemingly do not present themselves as such in the text. To press with questions [*presser de questions*], even if it is done without polemical haste, is already to imprint another text, to cross the marks of multiple writings and languages, to make repetition into an overprinting. Like the second blow of *Geschlecht* we will speak of later, this repetition can be good or bad. But the blow it bears, the marks it imprints, must they be regretted? There are two ways, at least, of writing *on* a text in order to let it appear. One consists in abstaining from any mark or remark, from any intrusion of writing that would risk covering over or disfiguring that which must precisely appear on its own, intact, naked. The other consists in . . . [Editors: The typescript abruptly stops here; what follows are several handwritten notes that are scarcely legible, which we attempt to decipher here.]—to press with questions → questioning essence of thought; at least as pathway → [? Place] (nor [? action, nor passion? but?] H. departs from this. There is one place—[??]—desire for place—to gather [in ink:] scene of *Geschlecht* (conf.: ??? ≠ aletheia/unconcealment).

11. Martin Heidegger, *Der Satz vom Grund* (*GA* 10), ed. P. Jaeger (1955–56; Frankfurt am Main: Vittorio Klostermann, 1997); *The Principle of Reason*, trans. Reginald Lilly (Bloomington: Indiana University Press, 1996).

recourse" here has limited relevance.[12] It would, then, be rather [*plutôt*] (and earlier [*plus tôt*], in a more initial, matutinal, eastern way) a question of a modest, discreet prerequisite, but one that is also formidably decisive for this entire classical system: what is a place, beyond or short of the geometric space of the *res extensa*, or even of being as *Vorhandenheit* in general? How to make one's way toward the locality (*Ortschaft*) of the place, toward the being-place of the place? This question is inseparable from that of a topology of being, such as will be prescribed, two years after the text on Trakl, in *Zur Seinsfrage* (1955), where Heidegger proposes an *Erörterung* of the line, questions the "place" of Nothingness and nihilism, and indicates the necessity, before any topography of nihilism, of a topology of being, of an attempt at "a situation of that site" (*die Erörterung desjenigen Ortes*), or place, that "gathers being and nothing into their essence, determines the essence of nihilism and thus lets us recognize those paths on which the ways towards a possible overcoming of nihilism emerge."[13]

We might say that "before" Being and Nothingness there is Place, that which gives rise [*donne lieu*] and makes it so that there is (*es gibt*) Being and Nothingness gathered together. If place is regularly, typically defined by gathering (*Versammlung*), our entire approach to the Heideggerian gesture will have to question this privilege of gathering and all that it entails.[14]

A discreet but decisive prerequisite, we were saying. But once this prerequisite no longer takes the form of a fundamental

12. S.V.: "Here we are, then, totally disarmed and without recourse."

13. Martin Heidegger, "Zur Seinsfrage," in *Wegmarken*, ed. Friedrich-Wilhelm von Herrmann (1976; Frankfurt am Main: Vittorio Klostermann, 2004), 412; "On the Question of Being," in *Pathmarks*, ed. and trans. William McNeill (Cambridge: Cambridge University Press, 2008), 311–12 (translation slightly modified).

14. Derrida's note: "The place gathers. Gathering shelters that which is gathered in the direction of its essence (*Der Ort versammelt. Die Versammlung birgt das Versammelte in sein Wesen*)," ibid., p. 386; "On the Question of Being," in *Pathmarks*, 292).

or transcendental requirement, we can no longer speak here of a simple regression toward conditions of possibility, but only of another approach, another pathway, and other *Wegmarken*. In relation to every criteriology or methodology, Heidegger allows that this path of thinking (*Denkweg*) may be errancy or aberrance (*Irrweg*).[15] He gives himself just one end from the opening lines of the text, an end that while not conflated with a finality, conclusion, or result, nevertheless does not amount to nothing: it is the "situation" of the place (*Erörterung*), "steps," a "path of thinking" that ends on, culminates in, opens onto (as you like) a question, once again a question that questions after the being-place of the place (*Ortschaft*). Of the place from which Trakl's speech proceeds—but it can proceed only by speaking—and however subtle or abstract this question may seem, it communicates with that of the idiom, habitat, then of nationality, and so on.[16] Here are the opening words:

> To situate (*erörtern*) here means first of all: to indicate the place (*in den Ort weisen*). It then means: to be attentive to the place (*den Ort beachten*). These two, to indicate the place and pay heed to it, are the preliminary steps to a situation (*die vorbereitenden Schritte einer Erörterung*). But we will have already shown enough daring (*wagen*) if, in what follows, we content ourselves with these preliminary steps. In a manner that corresponds to a path of though (*Denkweg*), the situation ends in a question (*endet* [. . .] *in eine Frage*). It questions towards the locality of the place.[17]

15. Heidegger, "Die Sprache im Gedicht," 33.

16. S.V.: "Here of the place from which Trakl's speech speaks, but you can see that, subtle or abstract though it may seem, this question is not unrelated to that of the idiom, habitat, nationality—and, as we will see, the human."

17. Heidegger, "Die Sprache im Gedicht," 33. In quotations throughout this edition we have followed Jacques Derrida's practice of placing Heidegger's original German text in parentheses whenever it is translated by

This last sentence looks at first, in the French translation, like a pointlessly heavy and laborious translation, an extravagant translation for "*Sie frägt nach der Ortschaft des Ortes.*"[18] The translators must have wanted to avoid resorting, as I did above, to "the locality of the place," a somewhat dry formula that risks suggesting that the essence of place, the locality, the being-place of the place is an abstract structure, a general condition of possibility or a formal essence. And it is true that *Ortschaft*, which also means being-place or essence of place, nevertheless retains a very concrete sense in everyday German (village or spot, but also locality). Heidegger no doubt wanted to retain this everyday sense, to maintain its presence in the designation of the very essence of place. This essence *takes place* and therefore has a singular, concrete, situatable place. But the French word "*localité*" also has two valences. Moreover, "*contrée*" has been used for a somewhat different region in the Heideggerian lexicon (*Gegend*, etc. . . .).[19] In any

---

the text immediately preceding it (for example, in the quotation above, "To situate (*erörtern*) . . ."); conversely, when Derrida gives Heidegger's German first, as happens on occasion, the translation is then placed in parentheses following it. As for Derrida's numerous interventions in the texts he quotes, we have indicated these in brackets.

18. Heidegger, 33. Derrida is referring to Jean Beaufret and Walter Brokmeier's translation of Heidegger's essay (see note 3 above). They render the sentence in question as "*Celle-ci questionne en direction de la contrée à laquelle appartient le site.*" (The latter questions in the direction of the region to which the place belongs.)

19. Derrida alludes here to paragraph 22 of *Being and Time*, where Heidegger defines "*Gegend*," a term the French translator Emmanuel Martineau renders as "*contrée*": "Ce 'vers où' de la destination outilitaire possible tenu d'avance sous le regard circon-spect de l'usage préoccupé, nous le nommons la contrée." The English translation by Joan Stambaugh renders the same passage in the following way: "This whereto of the possible belonging somewhere of useful things, which is circumspectly held in view in advance and in heedful dealings, we call the *region*." See Martin Heidegger, *Sein und Zeit* (1927; Tübingen: Max Niemeyer Verlag, 2006), 103; *Être et Temps*, trans. Emmanuel Martineau (Paris: Authentica, 1985), 92; *Being and Time*, trans. Joan Stambaugh (Albany: SUNY Press, 2010), 100.

case, the expression "in the direction" ("in the direction of the region") may also seem risky as a translation of "*nach*." Neither a view nor a direction is, in the strict sense, guaranteed or securely promised here. *Nach*: toward, after, as one *runs after* in order to follow; and that toward which one makes a commitment to take risks or give pledges did not wait to provoke. It has already called out, it already takes place. The question thus questions *after* [*d'après*] that which already takes place and shows itself, for example in the poem. The poem is there. Its being-there is that of the written or spoken *Dichtung*, but also, and already, of the unspoken *Gedicht* whose place is being sought after.

But as for the ultimate privilege of the questioning form that we might want to question and displace in turn (why should everything start or end with questions, in the form of a question?), we experience its singularity in its dependency with respect to the path, in the movement of the path (*Bewegung*), of the pathlike-character, of the being-path of thought, what Heidegger elsewhere calls the *Wegcharakter des Denkens*.[20] As path through and through, thought must search after (*nach*, toward), it must question *after* the place, which may come down to asking its way. But one must already be on the way in order to ask one's way. The *Bewegung* of the question is no doubt presupposed by every classical or modern problematic of reading, by hermeneutics, philology, poetics, etc. But this presupposition makes such problematics into derivative or conditioned moments.

Let us correct, then, a previous formulation. Heidegger does not give *himself* the end as a question. This question is given to him on the way (*unterwegs*), in the being-path of thought as the pathway *toward* but also *after* (*nach*) the given place. Because it is (on) the way, thought questions—and not the other way around.

---

20. See Martin Heidegger, *Frühe Schriften* (*GA* 1, *Nachwort*), ed. Friedrich-Wilhelm von Hermann (Frankfurt am Main: Vittorio Klostermann, 1978), 437.

(In his insistence on the step and the passage (*Schritt, Über-schritt*), and although he calls us back incessantly to the path and the walking movement (*Weg, Bewegung*) of thought, Heidegger never ventured to say of the foot what he says of the hand.[21] For Heidegger, we do not think or speak with the foot. Conversely, while he grew attached to the pair of shoes and their truth in painting, he never picked up, that I know of at least, Kant's glove.)[22]

We must not determine the questioning pathway as *research* or inquiry. *Epistēmē* and *historia* are particular modes, they derive from the pathlike [*cheminante*] essence of the question but are not conflated with it. The following paragraph puts them in their place, one might say. Under the guise of a clause of modesty, but with the authority of a verdict, Heidegger dismisses the human or social sciences on the threshold of this "situation." He names psychoanalysis (something he rarely does), alongside history, sociology, etc. Here I cite the French translation even though it is rather free and forgets the word "*historisch*":

> The situation undertaken here speaks of Georg Trakl only to contemplate (*bedenkt*) the site of his *Dict* (*den Ort seines Gedichtes*). For our time, which is hungry for information, biography, psychoanalysis, sociology, set as it is on the pure and simple extraction of formulas, such an approach (*Vorgehen*) remains, it is clear, unilaterally restricted, if not totally aberrant (*gar ein Irrweg*). The situation contemplates the site (*die Erörterung bedenkt den Ort*).[23]

21. See Derrida, "Heidegger's Hand (*Geschlecht* II),"

22. Immanuel Kant, *Prolegomena to Any Future Metaphysics*, trans. Gary Hatfield (Cambridge: Cambridge University Press, 2004), §13.

23. Heidegger, "Die Sprache im Gedicht," 33. In this instance, rather than translating Heidegger directly from the German, we have provided an English rendition of the French translation by Beaufret and Brokmeier to which Derrida is explicitly alluding here. A more literal translation of Heidegger's German would go as follows: "The placement speaks of Georg Trakl only so

Heidegger then proceeds from what he recalls as the origin, namely, the originary meaning of the German word "*Ort*." He will tell us in what sense *Erörterung* will have to orient itself as it orients thought toward the situation of the site. We will not rely only on the idiom of the word "*Erörterung*," so difficult to translate and as foreign to the everyday understanding of German as the French word "*situation*," in this active sense, may be to the French ear. We will have recourse to an originary sense, one indeed lost to usage, absent from standard dictionaries. This will be the sense of *Ort*, the place, which "originally (*ursprünglich*) designates [or signifies, *bedeutet*] the tip of the spear (*die Spitze des Speers*)."[24] *Ursprünglich*, that is to say, in our primitive language, and we are not far from Fichte here. But access to this language must be obtained first, and with a bound, for the origin is a leap (*Sprung*) and one never recovers it, in repetition, without beginning again. At the end of the introduction, it will be said of the poetic place that only a leap could, with one blow [*coup*], one glance [*coup d'œil*], open access to it ("*durch einen Blicksprung an den Ort des Gedichtes zu bringen*").[25] This leaping, sometimes elliptical and discontinuous approach is what literary critics, philologists, and philosophers reproach Heidegger for: he supposedly jumps arbitrarily in the middle of a poem, from one verse to another, from one poem to another without warning, without methodological caution. Heidegger knows this, he takes it on: blows, leaps, jumps, that's the rhythm and regime of this "reading" which does something other than "to read" and which remains simultaneously so slow, winding, cautious, lingering, retracing its steps, etc. But I have just named the themes

---

as to consider the place of his poem. For the age that has a historiographical, biographical, psychoanalytic, and sociological interest in naked expression, such a way of proceeding remains apparently one-sided, if not completely wayward. The placement considers the place." (—Trans.)

24. Heidegger, 33.
25. Heidegger, 33.

of this "situation": the leap, the blow (*Schlag*), the delay, the evening, etc.

Originally, then, the noun "*Ort*" designates the tip of the sword, spear, or javelin. Why bring this up? Heidegger devotes only one sentence to the weapon itself. It seems as though what matters to him is not the weapon, which can nevertheless be held in the hand (*zuhanden*), in one and sometimes two hands. Nor is it the symbol that one can display without putting a hand to it (monkeys and *Zugvogel* don't have hands, place even less so).[26] No, what matters and what will dominate this entire "situation" going forward is the motif of gathering (*Versammlung*), collection, convergence. *Ort*, the tip of the spear: the place toward which all the orienting forces of the weapon converge (*zusammenlaufen*) to gather there as in an indivisible point.[27] This point is not a properly geometrical point, and Heidegger does not use word "indivisible" that we will have to justify later on. But I insist on it because we are touching here upon what others would call the "axiomatic" of this "reading," words that I leave in scare quotes here for reasons alluded to above: there is or there must be gathering (*Versammlung*). It is one of the most frequent and decisive words in the text. Gathering gives rise to place [*donne lieu au lieu*] as singularity, it *gives* it its indivisible unicity.

> At the tip of the spear everything converges. The site gathers to itself [brings back or calls back to itself, *versammelt zu sich*, to itself, that is to say] toward the highest (*ins Höchste*) and outermost [*Äußerste*, to the limit of the outside, to the furthest limit, to the end of the tip].[28]

26. For Derrida's account of Heidegger's idiomatic play around the *Zug* of "*Zugvogel*," see p. 55, note 90. See Martin Heidegger, *Was heisst Denken?* (*GA* 8) (Frankfurt am Main: Vittorio Klostermann, 2002), 11.

27. Heidegger, "Die Sprache im Gedicht," 33.

28. Heidegger, 33.

Even though it situates (itself) at the limit between inside and outside, at the top of a thing that is also located between bodies and can run them through (Heidegger does not speak of this), this pointed place "penetrates and essences through everything else."[29] The tip passes through everything else, not because it pierces through the body of the enemy but, on the contrary (in the opposite sense, if you like), it ends and thus determines everything that converges toward itself. The tip traverses, then, the sword itself, or the spear, or the javelin, from the moment it is the gatherer (*das Versammelnde*). It brings back to itself as toward the place, it "safeguards what is drawn in." To safeguard [*garder*] here is *verwahren*, and each time it is a matter of guarding [*la garde*] there must be truth (*Wahrheit*). The truth of the sword, as with that of the poem, that which guarantees sense, orientation, guarding and the origin, is the extreme tip of the place. Such a guarding does not confine; the poem that keeps itself [*s'y garde*] there and first happens there does not for all that become hermetic, it does not take shelter in the enclosure of a hermeticism even if it appears secret and seems to require a hermeneutics. That which safeguards allows itself to be traversed, but it also traverses, passes through. What thus allows the passage, transparency, or translucency of daylight, its movement (*durch*) is always coupled with that of gathering: *Versammlung* and *durchscheinen, durchleuchten*.[30]

The tip of this weapon opens the way: on the first page, at the threshold of the "situation," it shows the place and gathers it in advance. It can leave you bewildered, or ironic. Some would also look to situate this tip: it also appears after, just after a paragraph that is very condescending about psychoanalysis, which might also have something to say about this "place," this place or figure. We can imagine Heidegger's retort: before you speak about a phallic symbol, make sure you know

29. Heidegger, 33.
30. Heidegger, 33.

what a tip in general means, what gathers there and above all the topological conditions that are always implied by psychoanalysis, in particular that which would make the phallus a major or transcendental signifier. This gesture is accompanied, especially in Lacan, by a topography. This topography presupposes a topology, the thought of what a place is. Before we know whether the extreme tip of a sword symbolizes a phallus or a phallic signifier, whether it, as a sign (*Zeichen*), shows (*zeigt*) anything at all or supports the chain of every other signifier, we must presume to know, and think, what *place* means, and what gathering in a place means.

What we are saying here about the sword could have been said earlier about the quill and what gathers itself, in handwriting, at the tip of the quill held in one hand. But that is not what's essential. It is not a matter of marking what a psychoanalytic theorization, for example that of Lacan, presupposes of the Heideggerian approach. It is not a matter of distinguishing them, and even less of setting them against each other. We would be led instead to interrogate what both discourses, basically in agreement on this point, and this tip, imply as to the *indivisibility* of the place, as to the gathering in the simplicity of the *Ort* or the letter. For Lacan, the letter is *the place* of the signifier. This is the explicit definition of that letter of which it is said, in the *Seminar on The Purloined Letter*, that it cannot be divided. The question I posed elsewhere on this point may be put, *mutatis mutandis*, to Heidegger.[31] The motif of gathering plays a decisive role, and everything is said, in a way, all the decisions have been made starting from this first page and this definition of place.[32]

The ironist would insist: Heidegger speaks blithely of the tip of the sword not only after getting haughty with psycho-

31. See Jacques Derrida, "Le facteur de la vérité," in *The Post Card: From Socrates to Freud and Beyond* (Chicago: University of Chicago Press, 1987), 411–96.

32. S.V.: "Is there place, and does one access this place through what converges there or through what may divide itself there?"

analysis but also at the opening of a text that one may be justified in reading as a great discourse on sexual difference, and
all that without seeming to suspect what the tip of a sword
could at the very least connote. Here, two hypotheses, between which I will not decide. One gives credit: Heidegger,
whom the thing would not have escaped, judged that a sly
wink would not only be silly, vulgar, and out of place, but
incompatible with what he had just said about psychoanalysis, about its scattered and derivative interests, its structural
blindness to what is at issue here. The irony would be on Heidegger's side, the most discreet and imperturbable, the most
assured irony. The other hypothesis, in spite of appearances,
would not be *philosophically* incompatible with the first. It is
the hypothesis of inadvertency, an attention little accustomed
to this type of thing, the inexperience that can push a person
not to see further than the end of his nose or his cane: for example in the milieu of political self-evidence.

Why insist on gathering [*rassemblement*], on the like [*sem-
blable*] that comes to gather a polysemic diversity in the simplicity of place? Heidegger does not intend here to situate the
idiom in general but this particular idiom, that of the poet and
of the particular "great poet," Trakl. "Great poet," those are
his words. "Every great poet (*Jeder große Dichter*) poetizes
solely (*dichtet nur*) from out of a unique poem (*aus einem einzigen Gedicht*)."[33] The unique (*einzigen*) marks the place in its
indivisible singularity, the absolute and inimitable propriety
[*propre*] of an idiom. And when Heidegger says "great poet,"
he is not giving in to some arbitrary triviality. He intends to
measure this greatness, or at least make it proportional to the
poet's devotion to his *Gedicht*. A poet is great only to the extent that he devotes himself, entrusts himself, gives himself
over to the unicity of this *Gedicht*, on the condition that he
devotes himself to it. I am not translating *Gedicht* into French,
especially not as "*Dict*," for reasons that will soon become

33. Heidegger, "Die Sprache im Gedicht," 33.

clear. "Greatness," Heidegger says, "is measured by [*bemißt sich*, in this way it is commensurate with] the extent to which the poet entrusts himself to this unique, in such a way that he is able to hold his poetizing saying purely within it (*sein dichtendes Sagen rein darin zu halten*)." If I do not translate *Gedicht*, especially not as "*Dict*," it is because Heidegger invites us to distinguish the *Gedicht* from the *dichtendes Sagen*, poetic speech or saying. In the absolute unicity of its idiom, the *Gedicht* is never said, it remains "unspoken." It is not to be mistaken for what the poet writes, says, delivers and publishes, with the multiplicity or entirety of his poems. The *Gedicht* is unsaid, unuttered, unspoken (*ungesprochen*): "*Das Gedicht eines Dichters bleibt ungesprochen*," which the French translation thinks it can render with "The poet's *Dict* is not disclosed by speech." The value of disclosure is foreign to this sentence, and Heidegger precisely places "speech" on the side of saying (*Sagen*): what remains "unspoken" is what does not belong to saying. The unspoken *Gedicht* must be distinguished from each poem, from all the poems that nevertheless speak or say it. It must be distinguished from everything that is said, even though it is not elsewhere, another thing in another place. None of the particular poems, nor the whole of the poetic "corpus," says the *Gedicht*, which it is necessary to understand here as a simplicity rather than an inexhaustible totality. And yet each poem speaks from it and says it each time.[34]

It is necessary, then, to hear this unsaid which, without being the unsaid that is repressed, barred, denied, speaks through all the poems that say it without saying it. A certain relationship of the flow or the wave (*Woge*) to the source (*Quelle, Ursprung*) suggests this passage from the unsaid to the poetic saying. It is something more and something other than a metaphor, and this figure must be made to fit with something Heidegger suggests about poetic rhythm, beyond the image that metaphysics portrays when it speaks in the name

34. Heidegger, 33.

of aesthetics. *Ruthmos* (Heidegger does not remind us of this here) also names in Greek an undulating and regular movement of water. The place of the poem is this unique and unspoken place from which each poem springs. The wave moves away from the source but without abandoning it. It does not become something else. The movement by which it springs (*entquellen*) but also frees itself from the source, its springing *from* the source flows back toward it, which is to say toward an ever "more concealed" origin: "The place of the poem, as the source of the moving wave [*der bewegenden Woge*, of the water's course], shelters the veiled essence [*das verhüllte Wesen*, the hidden essence] of what can initially appear as rhythm to metaphysico-aesthetic representational thinking (*dem metaphysisch-ästhetischen Vorstellen*)."[35] If one wants, then, to think rhythm beyond prosodic science, for example, if one is interested in the essence of rhythm as such, it is necessary to approach this place: between the unspokenness of the *Gedicht* and the saying of the poems, between the source and that which emanates from and then comes back to it. This double movement—the going, the return—this is a rhythm.

This essence of rhythm governs the order according to which a situation situates the place of the poem. Where to begin? That is always the question. And in which order to proceed? Heidegger justifies an order but, as the motif of rhythm and source suggests, this order is caught up in a circularity that recalls the "hermeneutic circle" we thought we could escape in one go, in the moment of the leap. Once the unicity of the *Gedicht* belongs to the unsaid, how do we access it? Of course, *on the basis of*, by starting from what is said in singular poems, in the occurrences of the *Gedicht*, which, after all, *does not exist* elsewhere, no more than a source exists in a separate state. One must explicate [*expliquer*], as they say, each poem. One must elucidate. This German word is as difficult to translate as the others: *Erläuterung*, which has often been

35. Heidegger, 34.

translated as "clarification," here as "elucidation." In everyday language, it refers to textual analysis or commentary. Heidegger here wants to awaken the light that is dormant in this word. "Elucidation brings *das Lautere* [the clear, the pure], which shines (*durchglänzt*) through everything that is said poetically, to a first appearance ["to its first splendor" says the French translation]."[36] What is clear, what is manifest, shows itself in what is pronounced in the poem—in other words, in its phenomenon—and this speaking may, or even must, be a singing. But the order of implications is this: "a correct elucidation (*eine rechte Erläuterung*) already presupposes the situation (*Erörterung*)."[37] Without prior access to the unique and indivisible place, the purity of the idiom, one could not begin to elucidate poetic texts: their wave proceeds—and this is rhythm itself—from the source that gives rise [*donne lieu*] to it. The occurrence of the poem would be unthinkable otherwise. The individual poem takes place only from the place that gives rise to it and toward which the individual poem signals in return. But here is the circle, and its form is classical: "conversely (*umgekehrt*), the situation (*Erörterung*) already requires [in order to access the place] that we pre-cursorily go through an initial elucidation of individual poems."[38] Heidegger does not call this a circle but—what seems to amount to the same thing—a relation of reciprocity (*Wechselbezug*). There must be convertibility or reversibility between *Erörterung* and *Erläuterung*. What we have there is a rhythm, and we might say that poetic rhythm, understood in its proper essence, dictates the rhythm of a correct "reading": this reading must be faithful to this alliance, this incessant conversion between *Erörterung* and *Erläuterung*. At bottom, those who would only see here a logical circle or methodological aporia would, simply, have understood nothing about the essence of

36. Heidegger, 34.
37. Heidegger, 34.
38. Heidegger, 34.

rhythm. But this incomprehension, this non-access are nothing other than metaphysical aesthetics: all of literary criticism, all of poetics, and so on.

Convertibility, conversion, we should also be able to say conversation: this is the movement, but also the place in which to dwell, the dwelling where dialogue perseveres (*verharrt*), a thinking dialogue, precisely, each thinking conversation (*jede denkende Zwiesprache*) with the *Gedicht*, which is to say the silence of a poet.[39] In the family of all the "two" words (*Zwiefalt, Zwietracht*, etc.), *Zwiesprache* names a two-way speech, speech exchanged here between *Denken* and *Dichten*. But this exchanged speech, which is not a trade or circulation, is exchanged, for the thinker as for the poet, with a *Gedicht* in its unspeakable place. It is necessary to persevere, stay, insist in this conversation with the poet's verses, but primarily with the unpronounced that gives the rhythm of verse, versification, its source. To persevere, dwell, *verharren*, can also be, according to the idiom of everyday German, *in Schweigen verharren*, to remain silent, to persevere in one's silence.

The French translation sometimes says "*entretien*" ["discussion"] and other times "*dialogue*" ["dialogue"] for this two-way speech (*Zwiesprache*) within which Heidegger introduces a new distinction. There are two essential modes of *Zwiesprache*, double language or double speech, two-way speech for a language [*langue*] that does not exist without speech [*parole*], outside of its occurrences. But the word "dialogue" attracts too many ambiguities; and since it is an essence of *Sprache*—at once language and speech—that it is a matter of thinking *in order to dwell in it*, let us be attentive to words that hold *Sprache* within them, for example *Zwiesprache* and *Gespräch*.

According to Heidegger there are, then, two essential modes of *Zwiesprache* when it perseveres in conversation with the silent *Gedicht* of the poet, turned toward it. The authentic

39. Heidegger, 34.

one, two-way speech properly speaking, "*die eigentliche Zwi-esprache*," with the poet must be poetic.[40] It is the *Gespräch* between poets who speak together and address one another as such, poetically. One can speak properly of the *Gedicht* only in a poetic mode that is, then, more than a mode or genre, and according to a speech that is not only poetizing but poetic (how, then, are we to translate *dichtende*?). But that does not exclude another *Gespräch*, one that is always possible and sometimes necessary, which relates *Denken* to *Dichten*. It is not a matter of philosophy but of thought, of thinking, we could say of the act of thinking if "act" were not charged with essential ambiguities, and if we, in the case of *Dichten*, had an appropriate verb in French.[41]

Such a *Gespräch* is, then, not the most authentic or the most appropriate, but it is possible and necessary. In their way, and in an indelible difference, thought and poetry have a "distinctive relation" to *Sprache*.[42] The French translation of *ausgezeichnetes Verhältnis* as "*rapport insigne*" restores the sign that this very common word still makes toward the sign. The *Gespräch* of thinking with poetry signals or receives its sign in this relation to the essence of *Sprache* that it aims to call, invoke, provoke, make come by means of the call (*her-vorzurufen*). But to call the being of language or speech can be done, like every call, only in the *Sprache* that already names itself, calls itself, marks itself, or signs itself in that *Gespräch* which is its own.

To what end does speech speak of itself in this way? To what end does it call in the call addressed to itself, to its essence? To what end is the *Gespräch* between thinker and poet? We find again here the problem of place, idiom, and habitation. The call takes place so that mortals—Heidegger does not yet say

40. Heidegger, 34.

41. S.V.: "Not of philosophy but of thinking with poetry, with the poetic act (wrong word) (impossible translation: the ordeal of this seminar)."

42. Heidegger, "Die Sprache im Gedicht," 34.

humans—"learn (*lernen*) again to dwell in *Sprache*."[43] Heidegger indeed says "again" (*wieder*). They no longer do it, then, they no longer dwell where they used to dwell, they have unlearned. The word "*lernen*" marks indeed the necessity of a new teaching. A learning is embarked upon in this proximity between thought and poetry, an experience of proximity that, in the case of Trakl,

> . . . has just barely begun. It requires a peculiar restraint [the soberest reservation] vis-à-vis Georg Trakl's poem. A thinking two-way speech with poetizing can serve the *Gedicht* only in a mediated way. For this reason, it runs the danger of rather disturbing the saying (*Sagen*) of the poem, instead of letting it sing from its own proper repose.[44]

Singing is the proper moment and possibility of the poem, of the *Gedicht* insofar as it comes to *Dichtung*. I don't know if the French word "*charme*," with its Latino-Valéryian resonance, translates *singen* without exporting it too much into the entirely different landscape of *carmen*. But ultimately, every translation into a Romance language bears the same sin.

We are still in the introduction, even before the beginning of the first part. At the threshold, the precautions multiply. Others would call these methodological. In fact, they warn us against method and methodologism. Not in the name of empiricism but, quite the contrary, in the name of a rigorous path toward the place. This path, which is not yet a methodical procedure, will no doubt seem arbitrary, capricious and doomed to improvisation as long as we have not situated, as Heidegger so often does elsewhere, the metaphysical project of method itself. The pre- or a-methodological precautions that are multiplied here, without being "questions of method,"

43. Heidegger, 34.
44. Heidegger, 34–35.

nevertheless outline limitations (*Beschränkungen*).⁴⁵ They de-limit all the more so as they refrain from all the discourses and bodies of knowledge that claim to authorize themselves with a method, to produce knowledge about a defined object and advance research or inquiry. To indicate the place of the *Gedicht*,

> ... does not present a poet's worldview, nor does it inspect his workshop [his place of work, *Werkstatt*]. Most of all, the "situation" of the *Gedicht* can never substitute for the listening of poems [it would not serve as their *Ersatz*], not even guide it.⁴⁶

The *Gedicht* is not a work; the poems outside of which it does not exist are speakable works, and it is necessary to hear their singing. A proposition in accordance here with an un-interrupted tradition: listening and singing are irreplaceable. Not only is the situation of the *Gedicht* not able to replace the irreplaceable, it cannot even claim to provide access to the poem. Heidegger does not claim to read (hence my suspicion with regard to this word), not even to teach how to read or speak, or even how to listen to the singing. "A thinking situation can render the listening question-worthy (*fragwürdig*) to the highest degree and, in the best of cases, more pensive [more contemplative, *besinnlicher*]."⁴⁷

This strategy of limitations is also, of course, a maneuver, in the best and worst sense of the word (let's leave this evaluative concern to Heidegger). It produces a double effect. Saying modestly: "Don't expect too much, anything else from this situation, etc.," it implies: "I reject in advance the methodological (scientific, epistemological, hermeneutic, poetical, historiographical, even philosophical) questions or objections

45. Heidegger, 34–35.
46. Heidegger, 34–35.
47. Heidegger, 34–35.

that might be raised in attributing to me a project that is not my own. From the place of these critiques, there is no chance of gaining access to what is essential."

Caught in the convertibility between situation and elucidation, Heidegger must make a choice if he wants to indicate the place. Two choices, even. As he recognizes, he must start from the poems that are actually written and not from the unspoken *Gedicht*: "*Hierbei müssen wir von den gesprochenen Dichtungen ausgehen.*" Heidegger does not make of this necessity a question. He makes one of the other choice, since he immediately asks, in a highly classical gesture: "The question remains: from which poems?"[48] For each of Trakl's poems shows, signals (*zeigt*), each one always orients itself toward the place of the *Gedicht*. What testifies (*bezeugt*) to this fact is the unique unison, consonance, resonance (*einzigartigen Einklang*) of the poetic works. This unity of the *Einklang* stems from the unity of the fundamental tone (*Grundton*). It belongs to the *Gedicht*, and from out of that which remains unspoken, the unity of this tone spreads like a rhythm to the wave of the poems. You'll recall that it is this fundamental tone, its very unity, that Heidegger wants to make us hear in the "*Ein*" (emphasized, *betont*) of "Ein *Geschlecht*." We can already say: in his *Gespräch* with Trakl, Heidegger lets himself be oriented by the hearing or the precursory listening of this "*Ein*" in "Ein *Geschlecht*." Such will have been the place. It will guide him in his choice of poems and particular verses in various poems, riddling the path with holes, setting up double bends, preparing the call or jumping-off point for each of the leaps, giving the movement for all the metonymic transitions. Heidegger knows that these choices will seem arbitrary or capricious (*willkürlich*) to those who speak in the name of competency or method only because they have no concern for, or even no idea of "place." "The choice is, however, guided by the aim to bring our attention, almost as though by means of a leap of

48. Heidegger, 34–35.

the eye [in a single leap, in a single 'glance,' with a leap of the look], to the place of the *Gedicht*."

This is the end of the introduction. Three preliminary pages, but to me everything seems decided already. In the following paragraph, after the "I," the first part illustrates and puts to work the decisive character of the *Blicksprung*: a line is quoted, without any additional preparation, without justification for the choice of line or even the choice of poem. It all starts like this, "One of the poems says":

> Es ist die Seele ein Fremdes auf Erden.[49]
>
> . . .
>
> It is, the soul, something strange on earth.[50]

The French translation adds the words "*en vérité*" ["in truth"] so that the line forms an alexandrine and in order to insist on the rhythm of the inversion.[51] "*Es ist die Seele*" . . . : yes, in truth, it is, the soul a stranger, something strange on earth. The quotation comes back four times over the course of twelve to thirteen pages of this first part. This is indeed an *Erläuterung*, a clarification or elucidation of this line. Other quotations will be mobilized, but as part of an approach that

49. Georg Trakl, "Frühling der Seele," quoted in Heidegger, "Die Sprache im Gedicht," 35.

50. Georg Trakl, "Springtime of the Soul II," in *Poems and Prose: A Bilingual Edition*, trans. Alexander Stillmark (Evanston: Northwestern University Press, 2005), 101. Our translations of Trakl here and throughout draw on Alexander Stillmark's translation of Trakl's poetry into English, though we have often found it necessary to modify this published translation—generally in a more literal fashion—in light of Heidegger's or Derrida's readings. Readers may wish to consult Stillmark's bilingual edition for both the German and the English versions of Trakl's verse; each time Trakl is cited here, we provide the page number for the German, followed by the English. Readers may also wish to consult the selection of Trakl's poetry translated by David Farrell Krell in the final pages of his *Phantoms of the Other*. (—Trans.)

51. The French translation of this line reads: "L'âme est en vérité chose étrange sur terre." (—Trans.)

is still preliminary. This first step remains indicative, it calls for a "second step"—this will be the second part.[52]

We must now change our rhythm and cease to follow the text sentence by sentence, as we have done up to this point. At the cost of a few violent moves and shortcuts, which I hope will open up some perspective, I will sometimes have to speed things up.

This first step leads us toward a gathering. There is place only in accordance with gathering (*Versammlung*). This now receives a name: *Abgeschiedenheit*. In everyday language, this means isolation, solitude, or separation, but also the condition of that which is departed, deceased, passed on, dead, departed toward death or separated by death, in death. As Heidegger speaks here of an *Abgeschiedenheit* that, precisely, does not mean "death" in the usual sense, the French translation has attempted to tie together all these connotations (departure, process of distancing, a passing on that is not one, death that is not a passing on) by forging or coining the word "*Dis-cès*" ["Dis-cease"]. He who is thus *abgeschieden*, dis-ceased, is the Stranger. If the sought-after site is always a place of gathering, "the whole saying of Georg Trakl's poems remains gathered (*bleibt versammelt*) unto the wandering Stranger (*auf den wandernden Fremdling*)," the wandering of a Stranger we won't call "nomadic": he is not countryless or destinationless.[53]

But in order thus to name the Stranger, his migration or departure, his *Abgeschiedenheit* as the proper place of the *Gedicht*, it is still necessary to think what "Stranger" means. It is in order to answer this question that this first step of the "situation" proceeds toward decease. This process goes through, among others, the questions of animality and *Geschlecht*.

What threads will we follow in this seemingly labyrinthine journey? First that of the word "stranger," which, appearing

52. Heidegger, "Die Sprache im Gedicht," 48.
53. Heidegger, 48.

in the first quoted line, lends the first step its entire movement: "*Es ist die Seele ein Fremdes auf Erden.*" Once again, the decision goes back to Old High German, which supposedly possesses the authentic signification of this word, "*fremd.*" Even before we get to this decision, let us underscore the paradox: the answer to the question of knowing what "stranger" means—or, rather, what "*fremd*" means, since translation already seems *a priori* illegitimate—remains idiomatic, it belongs to only one language, to a certain state of the language. The naming of the stranger, or rather of "*fremd,*" is so proper to a given idiom that the stranger *qua* stranger could not have access to it. And what one calls translation, in the usual sense, never crosses this border. We will ceaselessly see at work what one might call in German the *Unheimlichkeit* of this situation. Among all the senses it affects, there will be in particular the sense of "sense" (*Sinn, sinnan*).

How is the question "*Doch was heisst 'fremd'?*" called?[54] Everything begins with a kind of reversal of Platonism. When the first verse is quoted, we think on a first reading that we're in familiar territory: the earth, the earthly perishable, the soul, on the contrary, superterrestrial and imperishable, foreign to the earth. Isn't this Platonic doctrine? Let me quote a few lines from the French translation, which here fastidiously avoids the most salient words and stakes in the text (*Schlag, verschlagen*, etc.).

> Since Plato, the soul belongs to the supersensuous. If it appears in the sensuous, it is merely lost there. Here below, it is not in its element. It does not belong to the earth. In this world it is a strange thing.[55]

54. Heidegger, 36.
55. Heidegger, 35. The English here follows the French translation by Beaufret and Brokmeier quoted by Derrida, which reads: "L'âme appartient depuis Platon au suprasensible. Apparaît-elle dans le sensible, elle y est seulement égarée. Ici-bas, elle n'est pas dans son élément. Elle n'appartient pas à la terre. Elle est en ce monde chose étrange." A more literal translation

Now, the word for "lost" ["*égarée*"] is "*verschlagen*": at once separated, divided, partitioned, and stranded. Now, in the next sentence, translated in the French as "it is not in its element" ["*elle n'est pas dans son élément*"] Heidegger speaks of a "right strike" (*rechten Schlag*), an expression that will be used again later with reference to *Geschlecht*, to the two blows that come to strike the *Geschlecht*. The French translation will there translate as "*bonne frappe*" ["right strike"] what it leaves out here, purely and simply. What it renders with "Here below, it is not in its element" is "*Hier 'auf Erden' hat es mit ihr nicht den rechten Schlag.*"

So we think we can recognize in these lines the elements of "Plato's teachings": imprisoned in the body, the soul is a stranger there and should "leave the sensuous world, the world of that which is not truly and which is only the corruptible [what is being corrupted, *nur Verwesende*]."[56] This last word is important for us, because it will be reinterpreted later, in Trakl's text, in a non-Platonic way.

Now, Heidegger assures us that we find no trace of this metaphysical schema in the poem "Frühling der Seele" from which this verse is taken. Paying attention to this immediate context and to the way in which many other poems inscribe, imprint, strike the words that say the soul, or more properly the characters of the soul, its figures, Heidegger notices each time the same *Wortprägung*, the same type, the same stamp. And he gives nine examples of it: "The soul is something mortal, obscure, solitary, decrepit, ill, human, pale, dead, silent. This word coinage does not always have the same sense [. . .]."[57] The category of the stranger would be the most general, and

---

of Heidegger's German would read: "Since Plato's doctrine, the soul belongs to the supersensuous. If, however, the soul happens to appear in the sensuous, it is merely cast astray there. Here 'upon the earth' the soul is not in the right cast (*rechte Schlag*). It does not belong to the earth. Here, the soul is 'something strange.'"

56. Heidegger, 36.
57. Heidegger, 36.

"the soul, depicted in this manner, would merely be one case of the stranger among others (*ein Fall des Fremden unter anderen Fällen*)."[58] Whence the necessity of the question, a question that is not without interest for us who are interested in the idiom and nationality: "*Doch was heisst 'fremd'* (But what does 'stranger' mean)?" One could displace the sense of this question while maintaining the syntax, as Heidegger does with *Was heisst Denken?*: not "what does one call 'stranger' or what does 'stranger' mean?" but "what calls the 'stranger'?" or "what does the 'stranger' call?"[59] Although Heidegger does not do this explicitly, the sense of his meditation allows or calls for this displacement.

In any case, Heidegger poses this question only on the basis of German, and High German. He excludes any consideration of another language. What does that mean? First, in all likelihood, he thinks he must remain within the borders of German in order to say what must be thought of the stranger, to call it—which is quite normal—but also in order to say what is called stranger, what calls the stranger or what the stranger calls. This means, next, that the meaning is inseparable from the language, a familiar theme. But beyond these two obvious meanings, the absence of any reference to a foreign language (Latin, Italian, Spanish, French, or even English) has another significance: thus excluded is everything in "*étranger*" (*straniero, extraño*, strange, etc.) that shares in the Latin *extraneus*: what is outside and thus presupposes the border, or even a given opposition between an outside and an inside. Now, "*fremd*" neutralizes this opposition; its essential signification supposedly no longer needs it. One can be a stranger or foreigner (*fremd*) on the inside.

> One habitually understands by "strange" [Heidegger notes] that which is nonfamiliar [the non-intimate, *das Nichtvertraute*] and does not speak [does not speak to you, is not

58. Heidegger, 36.
59. Heidegger, *Was heisst Denken?*, 117.

addressed to you, *was nicht anspricht*], something which is rather cumbersome and disquieting. [But, once again, we must have recourse to what the word signifies properly (*bedeutet eigentlich*).] [. . .] However, strange (*fremd*)— Old High German "*fram*"—properly means: ahead towards elsewhere [toward another place of destination, over there, ahead, making its way], on the way to . . . (*unterwegs nach*), towards what has been held in store in advance (*dem Voraufbehaltenen entgegen*).[60]

Unterwegs, which appears in the title of this volume, *Unterwegs zur Sprache*, might gather together the crux of what is said in this text on Trakl. The title in its entirety, as well, since, as we shall see, it is also toward the *Sprache* and the right strike of language or speech in its very essence that everything proceeds. *Unterwegs* also gives two of Trakl's poems their titles, the second of which has two versions.[61]

Thus the stranger (but we would have to say only *das Fremde*, from now on) peregrinates, migrates (*wandert*). He does so in advance, forward, by anticipating, and that's what is important here: "*Das Fremde wandert voraus.*"[62] For this peregrination is not a straying; even less is it a nomadic state.

The stranger does not err [*es irrt nicht*, he is not lost, astray, without a proper path], he has a destination [*Bestimmung*, he is also searching for a place, like, in short, the thinker who searches for the place in his *Gespräch* with the poet— and it's the same approach]. [. . .] The stranger, [even though he is] himself barely disclosed to himself, already follows a call (*Ruf*) to the way toward his proper (*folgt . . . dem Ruf auf den Weg in sein Eigenes*).[63]

60. Heidegger, "Die Sprache im Gedicht," 36–37.
61. Georg Trakl, *Das dichterische Werk*, ed. Walther Killy et Hans Szklenar (Munich: Deutscher Taschenbuch Verlag, 1972), 48, 169–70.
62. Heidegger, "Die Sprache im Gedicht," 37.
63. Heidegger, 37.

One could speak of repatriation [*repatriement*] if the French word "*patrie*" did not call up reservations we will come back to later. But the movement toward the proper is without a doubt a movement of return, even if the return remains an adventure. Starting from the Old German "*fram*," toward which one has returned as if headed for what is proper to the language, the semantics of "stranger" have been profoundly displaced— and in the direction of that which responds, precisely, to the call that leads it back toward its proper, its "home," toward its proper destination (*Bestimmung*). This displacement that effects *in* language that which language will have spoken of— the return toward the proper that a call destines one for—has, then, moved us away from the everyday sense of "stranger," as much in our Latin languages as in everyday German. The everyday sense has made itself strange to the sense of "*fremd*," to its proper sense.

Starting from this semantic reappropriation, the interpretation of Trakl's verse changes sense and direction.[64] It becomes anti-Platonic. But this inversion refers to "Plato's doctrine," and the French translation should have marked it rather than rendering "*seit Platons Lehre*" as "since Plato."[65] For, beyond or on this side of "doctrine," we can imagine a reading of Plato's text that would submit it to the same gesture of reinterpretation and shield it from "Platonism." But let's move on. If the soul is a stranger on earth, that does not mean that it is a stranger to the earth. On the contrary, here we find the

64. S.V.: "Starting from this semantic displacement—which consisted, let it be noted, in making the word '*fremd*' a *fremdes*, a stranger that one has made answer to his original or originary and final destination by repatriating it toward its proper, namely, its signification in Old German, *fremd* having become a foreign word that needed only to answer the call by being called back to its proper, and Heidegger brought it back home toward its proper (a doubling that would be necessary to insist on . . .)—starting from this semantic displacement which is a repatriation of the stranger, of the word 'stranger' toward its destination, the interpretation of Trakl's verse will literally change sense [*sens*] and direction; indeed, it will be anti-Platonic."

65. Heidegger, "Die Sprache im Gedicht," 35.

migrant (*fremd*) on the way toward the earth. "It does not flee the earth, it seeks (*sucht*) it" as its destination, in order to dwell in it poetically and save it.[66] As he will say later of *das Land* (we'll have to come back to this), it is a place that is what it is only insofar as it *promises* dwelling.

It is not enough to say that the soul is on its way toward the earth to locate its proper essence there, drawn in this way toward its essence. The trait that draws it in this way (*Zug*) is a fundamental trait, its very characteristic, its *Grundzug*. The fact that the soul belongs in this way to the earth does not yet tell us *toward where*, on earth, the stranger's step is called. In keeping with a typical gesture that will no doubt seem exorbitant with respect to certain norms of exegesis or literary criticism, Heidegger responds with another poem, a "stanza from the third part of 'Sebastian im Traum.'"[67] How is this leap to another poem—to find the answer to a question one thinks one hears in the first poem—justified? First of all, no doubt, by the presupposition that all the poems say the same thing, the unique and gathering *Gedicht*, which itself remains unspoken. This is part of the *Erörterung*. But the clarification of poems, their *Erläuterung*, requires another justification as soon as we are caught up in the convertibility (*Wechselbezug*) between *Erörterung* and *Erläuterung*. Heidegger practices then what I will call, not without hesitation, a metonymic transition.[68] I hesitate to use these words because Heidegger would most likely see in them recourse to a rhetorical knowledge confident in its technique and its categories in this place

66. Heidegger, 37.
67. Heidegger, 37.
68. S.V.: "The only apparent justification for this leap, this jump to another poem to answer a question left open by another, is, in addition to the general presupposition that all the poems of the great poet say the same and unique and gathering *Gedicht*, it seems to me (if I'm not mistaken) that the only justification from the point of view of the *Erläuterung* if not the *Erörterung* (*Wechselbezug*) is a sort of metonymic transition, namely, the presence in the poem to which it abruptly asks for an answer to the question of the other poem—the presence, then, of the word '*ein Fremdes.*'"

where rhetoric itself must be interrogated as a derivative moment of metaphysics. But I'm keeping these words as a preliminary indication—let's say, a metonymic indication. Heidegger draws his argument, then, from the presence in *another* poem of the words "*ein Fremdes.*" But around these words there is something else, at least two other things that will lead to the answer: the noun *Untergang*, decline, descent, downward movement, and the adjective *blau*, the azure color that will go on to play a decisive role in the metonymic constellation of the entire "reading":

> O wie stille ein Gang den blauen Fluß hinab
> Vergessenes sinnend, da im grünen Geäst
> Die Drossel ein Fremdes in den Untergang rief.[69]

I will first quote the published translation:

> O how tranquil to walk down by the blue river
> Pondering forgotten things, when in the green branches
> The thrush called a strange thing into decline.[70]

What I referred to as a metonymic link is also a jump. In the style of commentary, the next sentence replaces the stranger with the soul: "*Die Seele ist in den Untergang gerufen* (the soul is called into decline)."[71] We can't say this is wrong, but nothing "explains" this substitution.[72] Likewise, when he specifies that the "decline" is not a fall, a catastrophe or a collapse, Heidegger proceeds by way of a jump and a metonymy that are just as quick. He appeals to a third poem, "Verklärter Herbst," which also speaks of *untergehen*, and of an *Untergang* that

---

69. Trakl, "Sebastian im Traum," quoted in Heidegger, "Die Sprache im Gedicht," 37.

70. Trakl, "Sebastian in a Dream," in *Poems and Prose*, 50/51.

71. Heidegger, "Die Sprache im Gedicht," 38.

72. S.V.: "I'm not saying this is wrong, but there is a metonymy here that is not explained in the sense of *Erläuterung*."

seems foreign to all negativity. Indeed, it leads toward repose and silence. This is the last line:

> Das geht in Ruh und Schweigen unter.[73]
> . . .
> It goes down in repose and silence.[74]

The French translation should have perhaps avoided the word "*sombrer*" ["to sink"], the connotation of which retains something negative.[75]

"Which repose? That of the dead. But which dead ones? And in which silence?" Heidegger then asks, returning to the first poem, once again citing "*Es ist die Seele ein Fremdes auf Erden*" so as to search in the subsequent lines the answer to the questions posed, in short, by the answer of the other two poems. Some might consider this a singular approach.[76] "The stanza continues as follows:"[77]

> . . . Geistlich dämmert
> Bläue über dem verhauenen Wald . . . [78]
> . . .
> . . . Spiritually in twilight,
> Blue upon the clear-cut forest . . . [79]

Bläue, the noun, refers to azure, the blue of the sky. It "twilights" (*dämmert*). Twilight arrives when day breaks or night falls. The bluing twilight, as a spirit, as spirit, marks the declining

73. Trakl, "Verklärter Herbst," quoted in Heidegger, "Die Sprache im Gedicht," 38.

74. Trakl, "Transfigured Autum," in *Poems and Prose*, 10/11.

75. The French translation reads: "Cela va sombrant dans le repos et le silence."

76. Heidegger, "Die Sprache im Gedicht," 38.

77. Heidegger, 38.

78. Trakl, "Frühling der Seele," quoted in Heidegger, "Die Sprache im Gedicht," 38.

79. Trakl, "Springtime of the Soul II," in *Poems and Prose*, 100/101.

of the sun that has just been mentioned. It is a question of both the course of the day and that of the year: a few pages further on, Heidegger will bank on an etymology that will secure a great coherence for his entire course [*démarche*], which is that of the sun itself: "To walk (*gehen*), *ienai*, means in Indo-European: *ier*—the year (*das Jahr*)." Such is the coming-and-going movement (*Gang, Aufgang, Untergang*) of the sun.[80]

Walking and the declining (*Neige*) of the day, the year, an attention to seasons and twilights, all this motivates or justifies a new "metonymy," the call to *another* poem, the title of which speaks the decline of a season, "Sommersneige." The "metonymy" passes by way of blue, the adjective or the noun, the color or the sky (metonymy of azure). It gathers a potent constellation of motifs that will dominate the entire "situation," namely, "the step of the stranger," the "game" (an animal that happens to be blue), and memory retained.

> Der grüne Sommer ist so leise
> Geworden und es läutet der Schritt
> Des Fremdlings durch die silberne Nacht.
> Gedächte ein blaues Wild seines Pfads,
> Des Wohllauts seiner geistlichen Jahre![81]

> The green summer has grown so quiet
> And the stranger's step rings
> Through the silver night.
> Would that a blue game retained the memory of its path,
> Of the harmony of its spiritual years![82]

In the French translation, we read "*si discret*" ["so discreet"] in place of "*so leise*." These words always recur, as Heidegger

---

80. Heidegger, "Die Sprache im Gedicht," 43.

81. Trakl, "Sommersneige," quoted in Heidegger, "Die Sprache im Gedicht," 39.

82. Trakl, "Summer's Decline," in *Poems and Prose*, 94/95.

[38] *Geschlecht III*

notes, in Trakl's poems. "We tend to believe that '*leise*' simply means: scarcely sensible to the ear."[83] Now, "*leise* means slowly (*langsam*)," gently, and to remind us of this Heidegger once again has recourse to the old word *gelisian*: it means to slide (*gleiten*).[84] Without hazarding a translation of "*das Leise ist das Entgleitende*," let us say that it is what one barely hears, gentle slowness, what slides, what escapes discreetly by sliding away, what passes imperceptibly without being noticed, by effacing its limits. "Summer slides away thus into autumn, the evening of the year."[85]

This inaudible sliding describes the movement of metonymy. Heidegger leads us by sliding from one poem to another, from one line to another, following the incline or the turn of a word: a password stepping in discreetly each time in the inclination, and it is the inclination that calls the shots; it is what speech speaks of in this *Gespräch*.

Sliding from one place to another, a series of questions orients us here toward the assimilation of the "blue game" into a "gentle animal" (*sanfte Tier*). Metonymy steps in between many poems, and we cannot follow it here, but each time, in two pages, it's: "in another poem . . . ," "another poem sings . . . ," "another poem says . . . ," "elsewhere . . . ," etc.[86] Let us follow only the quite important track of the animal. The animal (*Tier*) here possesses an animality (*Tierheit*) that has nothing bestial (*tierisch*) about it, insofar as this entails brutality or violent savagery. This animal, says Heidegger, is probably (*vermutlich*) not bestial.[87] For, it can retain in memory what it sees, for example, the path of the stranger. It is through this retention, this retained memory or this retaining memory, that the animality in question will distinguish itself from simple bestiality. Nevertheless, "this animality still wavers in

83. Heidegger, "Die Sprache im Gedicht," 39.
84. Heidegger, 39.
85. Heidegger, 39.
86. Heidegger, 40.
87. Heidegger, 41.

a certain indetermination (*im Unbestimmten*)."[88] It was with this decisive passage in view that I thought it was necessary to precede this "reading" with that of other Heidegger texts[89] on animality.[90] The indetermination of the animal stems from the fact that:

> This animality has not yet been brought into [brought back, gathered, *eingebracht*, "*recueillie*" ["collected"] says the French translation], into its essence [into its proper being, *Wesen*]. This animal [Heidegger continues without hesitation], namely, the thinking animal (*nämlich das denkende*), the *animal rationale*, the human, as Nietzsche puts it, has not yet been firmly set (*fest gestellt*).[91]

88. Heidegger, 41.

89. See Derrida, "Heidegger's Hand (*Geschlecht* II)."

90. S.V.: "It is because of this wavering and this indetermination that, in this seminar, I started off this reading with the questions you're familiar with concerning the ape and the human, the determination of animality in *Was heisst Denken?* A letter I have since received—which was of great interest to me, including the disguise of its signature, 'Saint Jean d'août'—reminded me, among other things, of a reference Heidegger makes in *Was heisst Denken?* to an animal, in this case a migratory bird. I was familiar with this allusion, which incidentally is located in the lecture course itself and not in the transition I read, and it also precedes, already, a long reference to Hölderlin's *Mnemosyne*. If I did not quote it, this is because it is more elliptical than the reference to the ape, it does not have to do with the hand, and especially because it philosophically says exactly the same thing and even more, I hesitate to say brutally, but more assertively, namely, that we are animals but we are not beasts. Here is the sentence, it concerns this withdrawal, you'll recall, this draw of withdrawal (*Zug des Entziehens*) in the face of which Socrates did not take shelter, and Heidegger writes: 'When we enter the draw of withdrawal (*Zug des Entziehens*), we draw towards [. . .]— only in an entirely different way than migratory birds [*nur ganz anders als die Zugvögel*, the allusion is obviously motivated by the fact that the migratory bird is called *Zugvogel*, and thus by the presence of the word *Zug* in the name of this bird]—what draws us in as it withdraws itself.' So, there, too, there is an abyss—'in an entirely different way'—between the beast and us." See Martin Heidegger, *What Is Called Thinking?*, trans. J. Glenn Gray (New York: Perennial Library, 1976), 9 (translation modified).

91. Heidegger, "Die Sprache im Gedicht," 40.

We will return later to this reference to Nietzsche and to a particular passage from *Was heisst Denken?* concerning, precisely, the passage (*Übergang*) from man to *Übermensch* and the determination of the *animal rationale* as a grasping human (*vernehmen*) or, once again, as the human of grasping reason (*Vernunft, vernehmen*). As in the case of the *Greiforgane* of the ape, Heidegger opposes the grasp to the gift in order to *define* animality. Here, the retention of memory, which defines the "thinking" animal and distances it from simple bestiality, is supposedly not of the order of grasping, seizing, or reasoning.

When Nietzsche says that the human has not yet been set, fixed (*fest gestellt*), he does not mean it in the sense of something not yet "established" (*konstatiert*) as a fact:

> This he is in all too decided a manner. This means: the animality of this animal has not yet been brought into something firmly secured (*ins Feste*), that is to say [Heidegger translates], *nach "Haus," in das Einheimische ihres verhüllten Wesens gebracht* (reached "home," "at home," the intimate hearth of its concealed essence).[92]

A certain repatriation has not yet taken place, for the path of this destination is a path of return, even if the future itself, the chance of the future, here plays itself out as the riskiest adventure. The lexicon of house, homeland, or hearth does not give rise to [*donne lieu*] images or metaphors. I have attempted to explain this elsewhere, as the catastrophe of metaphor, and since this concerned Heidegger, precisely, I won't insist on it.[93]

> It is around firmly setting [*Fest-stellung*, this setting up or repatriation] this essence that Western-European

92. Heidegger, 40.

93. Jacques Derrida, "The *Retrait* of Metaphor," in *Psyche: Inventions of the Other*, vol. 1, ed. Peggy Kamuf and Elizabeth Rottenberg (Stanford, CA: Stanford University Press, 2007), 48–80.

metaphysics since Plato perhaps turns. Perhaps it turns in vain [Heidegger adds]. Perhaps for it the way (*Weg*) to the "on-the-way" (*in das "Unterwegs"*) remains blocked. The animal which has not yet been firmly set in its being is the human of today. [This is who Trakl poetically names the "blue game," this is the mortal who remembers the stranger and would like to come back "home," to the hearth of human essence.][94]

Few are those who undertake this peregrination, they remain unknown because "what is essential comes about (*sich ereignet*) in silence, in a sudden and rare way."[95] When it does come about, when the traveler "arrives at the door" (another poem, "Ein Winterabend"),[96] it is because the blue game, "where and when it essences (*west*), has abandoned (*verlassen*) the present form of the human essence (*die bisherige Wesengestalt*)."[97] The alternative here is marked between *wesen* (the verb) and *verwesen* (to break down, decompose, lose its essence), as well as between *wesen* and a series of verbs marking, with *ver-*, downfall (*verfallen*) or loss (*verlieren*): "Yesterday's human decays (*verfällt*) to the extent that he loses (*verliert*) his essence (*Wesen*), that is, decomposes (*verwest*)."[98] The essential form of yesterday's human decomposes (in the everyday sense of the term, that of the cadaver, even though Heidegger will go on to displace this signification) to the extent that it dislocates itself from its essence (*Wesen*), disessences itself, as it were.[99]

94. Heidegger, "Die Sprache im Gedicht," 41–42.
95. Heidegger, "Die Sprache im Gedicht," 41–42.
96. Trakl, "Ein Winterabend," quoted in Heidegger, "Die Sprache im Gedicht," 42.
97. Heidegger, "Die Sprache im Gedicht," 42.
98. Heidegger, 42.
99. S.V.: "The translation here is impotent when it comes to rendering the series of verbs beginning with *ver-* (which all indicate a movement of de-, a negative movement of decomposition, dispossession, dismantling, disposal: '*Der bisherige Mensch verfällt, insofern er sein Wesen verliert, d.h.*

[42] *Geschlecht III*

But this decomposition, this *Verwesen*, is not simply that of putrefaction in death. Over the course of an itinerary that I cannot follow here step by step, Heidegger quotes several times from "Siebengesang des Todes": "*O des Menschen verweste Gestalt*."[100] "Seven is the sacred number."[101] Previously, azure had been referred to as sacred insofar as it collects and gathers (*versammelt*).[102] Whether it's a matter of place, azure, or stone, the value of gathering (which gathers this entire *Gespräch*, and on which we are thus placing the weight of our question) is always associated with the sacred, but also with appeasement, gentleness, with what will transform the two of dissension (*Zwietracht*) according to the promise of a two without war (*Zwiefalt*). Sung under the sign of the sacred, seven or death does not signify here the end of life but the decline toward which the stranger is called. "This death is not a decomposition (*Verwesung*) but the abandoning of the [already] decomposed form of the human (*der verwesten Gestalt des Menschen*)."[103] "*O des Menschen verweste Gestalt* . . ."

The meditation on this decomposed form passes by way of various places around which one should dwell, the nocturnal lake, the selenic voice (*mondene Stimme*) of the sister, whose figure haunts Trakl's entire oeuvre and which announces the couple of this gentle sexual difference: between brother and

---

verwest.' The French translation plays on *poser* and *décomposer*: 'The old man breaks down to the extent that he deposits his being, in other words, decomposes,' yes, but there is no 'pose' there (except further on where the French translation does not call upon it, strangely). The most important thing is the relation between *wesen* and *verwesen*, which will play an ongoing role throughout the remainder of the text."

100. Trakl, "Siebengesang des Todes," quoted in Heidegger, "Die Sprache im Gedicht," 42; Trakl, "Sevenfold Song of Death," in *Poems and Prose*, 86/87. This line reads in English: "O the decayed figure of Man." (—Trans.)

101. Heidegger, "Die Sprache im Gedicht," 42.

102. Heidegger, 40.

103. Heidegger, 42.

sister.[104] With some regret, I hasten toward the conclusion of this first part. What is said there of *Geschlecht* will have magnetized our entire reading. This reading, as I announced, proceeds slowly yet must still go sifting, hunting, tracking.

The four verses of "Herbstseele," at the point where Heidegger quotes them, name once again game and blue. We can perhaps hear them more distinctly from this point forward when the animal withdraws by sliding away (*entgleitet*):

> Bald entgleitet Fisch und Wild
> Blaue Seele, dunkles Wandern
> Schied uns bald von Lieben, Andern.
> Abend wechselt Sinn und Bild.[105]

> Soon fish and game slide away.
> Blue soul, darksome wandering.
> Soon severed us from loved ones, others.
> Evening alters sense and image.[106]

What of Others (*Andern*) in this poem? For Heidegger, no doubt about it, Others figure the decomposed form, the decomposition of humanity, or more precisely the blow or the stock, the strike or the type (*der Schlag*) that impresses upon this sort of depressed—let's not say degenerate—form. And once again we find the recourse to "our language" in a passage I already quoted,[107] which we will read again now in a more determined context:

---

104. S.V.: "See Hegel, the sister who has a relation without desire to the brother. Much to be said when it comes to Trakl, but we cannot for the moment dedicate to this all the time it would deserve."

105. Trakl, "Herbstseele," quoted in Heidegger, "Die Sprache im Gedicht," 73.

106. Trakl, "Autumn Soul," in *Poems and Prose*, 66/67.

107. Derrida, *Psyche*, 2:53.

The wanderers who follow the Stranger find themselves immediately severed (*geschieden*) from the "loved ones," who are "others" for them. Others—this is the stock of the decomposed form of the human. Our language calls *Geschlecht* the human essence (*Menschenwesen*) that has received the stamp of a strike (*aus einem Schlag geprägte*) and that, in this strike, has been struck with specification (*und in diesen Schlag verschlagene*). [As we recalled, *verschlagen* means "specified" in the sense of separated, cloistered, dissociated; and the adjective *verschlagen* also means cunning, sly, clever. Heidegger continues:] The word means humankind (*Menschengeschlecht*) in the sense of humanity (*Menschheit*), as well as species (*Geschlechter*) in the sense of trunks, stocks, and families, all of that struck once again in the twofold of the sexes (*dies alles wiederum geprägt in das Zwiefache der Geschlechter*). The species (*das Geschlecht*) of the "decomposed form" (*der "verwesten Gestalt"*) of the human the poet calls the "decomposing" species (*das "verwesende Geschlecht"*). This species is set outside of its way of being and is thus the "upset" species.[108]

The French translation, which above had recourse to the word "*dépose*" to translate "*verliert*," does not use it here at the very moment the text underscores the *setzen*: "*Es ist aus der Art seines Wesens heraugesetzt und darum das 'entsetzte' Geschlecht*," thus authorizing the logic of a quotation.

We had already read this passage. What does the rest of the text have to tell us that's new, if we can put it like that? It will say something new [*de nouveau*] about the "once again" ["*de nouveau*"] (*wiederum*) that once more re-marks what comes to be marked in or as the duality of sexes: sexual difference.[109]

---

108. Heidegger, "Die Sprache im Gedicht," 45–46.
109. S.V.: "*Geschlecht* is struck two times: once in general: human species, stock, family, and so on, then struck a second time, as all of that by and in sexual difference, as sexual difference."

There are, then, two blows, two strikes, two stamps. A first blow strikes to leave its stamp, or rather to constitute with its stamp a "first" *Geschlecht*. But the second blow seems bad. It is an evil, it is evil itself. Heidegger will speak of evil (*das Böse*) only later in the text. For the moment, he names the curse (*Fluch*), no doubt as an implicit reference to a Trakl verse he does not quote: "*O des verfluchten Geschlechts*," we read in *Sebastian im Traum* (*Traum und Umnachtung*). The blow that strikes the species is the curse: "With what is this species (*Geschlecht*) struck (*geschlagen*), that is to say, cursed (*verflucht*)?"[110] Why does the French translation here prefer the word "*plaie*" ["wound"] for "*Fluch*" and "struck with some wound" for "*verflucht*"? So as to avoid the religious connotation? But in rejecting any Christianizing interpretation of Trakl, Heidegger will not look, further on, as we shall see, to deny the Christian signification of his lexicon, or even less so the equivocality that it entails. Attempting to efface this equivocality is not only futile, it denatures the text itself, Trakl's text and Heidegger's. Is it the mention of the Greek *plēgē* that—this is another hypothesis—attracted the word "*plaie*" in advance? This would not be enough to justify the erasure of all the connotations attached to the word "curse" [*malédiction*] and the word "*Fluch*," for which it is, in fact, the only possible translation, aside from perhaps "blasphemy" in other contexts.

> Curse (*Fluch*) in Greek is called *plēgē*, our word "*Schlag*."
> The curse of the decomposing species (*des verwesenden Geschlechtes*) consists in the fact that this old species is struck apart (*auseinandergeschlagen*) into the discord of the sexes (*in die Zwietracht der Geschlechter*).[111]

110. Heidegger, "Die Sprache im Gedicht," 46.
111. Heidegger, 46.

Zwietracht, discord, duel, is the becoming-war of a duality or duplicity (*Zwiefalt, Zwiefache*), which is not itself cursed. *This* sexual, befallen, second, cursed difference—this is the bad blow brought upon the species or the sex, on the *Geschlecht*. A certain *Trachten* will continue to work in the text after this. *Trachten jenem nach dem Leben* means to go after someone's life, to make an attempt on someone's life. What the French translation renders as "On the basis of this (*die Zwietracht der Geschlechter*) each of the two genders [the two sexes] rushes into the unbridled state of game, a desolate savagery reduced to itself,"[112] is *"Aus ihr trachtet"*: rushes, hurls itself, strives for . . . Strives for what, in short? To become savage and bestial again, merely game.

Here now is the formula that seems to me to carry the force and enigma of the text, the premises of which I attempted to indicate[113] in the Marburg lecture course (1928): "Not the two-fold as such, but rather discord is the curse (*Nicht das Zwiefache als solches, sondern die Zwietracht is der Fluch*)."[114] Sexual difference is not cursed, only that which determines it in *opposition*, war, or division.[115] Does this start with Adam and Eve? With Platonism? With Christianity? The answer: later.

The end of the paragraph defies translation more than ever. It multiplies the strikes, the words from the "family" of *schlagen, Geschlecht*, and its generation: *verschlagen*, to separate, *zerschlagen*, to break, shatter, dismantle. This lexico-semantic

112. Heidegger, 46. The French translation here reads: "À partir d'elle, chacun des deux genres se rue à l'effrénement de la sauvagerie, désolée et réduite à elle-même, du gibier." A more literal translation of Heidegger's German would be "From out of this discord, each of the sexes strives after the unbridled turmoil of an always individuated and sheer wildness of the wild." (—Trans.)

113. See Derrida, *"Geschlecht I."* For the "Marburg lecture course," see Heidegger, *Metaphysische Anfangsgründe der Logik im Ausgang von Leibniz.*

114. Heidegger, "Die Sprache im Gedicht," 46.

115. S.V.: "Let us translate: it is not even difference in *Geschlecht*, thus also a certain sexual difference, which is cursed, but a determination of this difference in opposition, thus in war and division."

"family" imports, in what is irreducible in its idiom, two inseparable connotations. First of all, it is that which hurts [*fait mal*] in a blow: the strike hurts [*la frappe fait mal*], evil strikes [*le mal frappe*], one thinks automatically (why?). Next, it is that which writes by striking, typography, the graphic stamp and imprint. And so [*du coup*], with the second blow [*du deuxième coup*] writing becomes evil. There is a good and bad strike, a good and bad writing. I will attempt to demonstrate later on that, despite Heidegger's insistent protestation, this gesture remains more Platonic and more Christian than it may seem. As is the case for Plato, there is a good and bad writing, the misfortune—and the chance—stemming from the fact that the one repeats the other, indissociably.

We won't dare say that there is a good and bad blow. But there is a "right blow," a "right strike," and there is a second curse that is affected with bad sexual difference, sexual war. "It [discord, *Zwietracht*] carries the species (*Geschlecht*), on the basis of the turmoil of blind savagery, into division (*Entzweiung*) and separates it [and not 'misplaces' ['*égare*'] it, as the French translation has for *verschlägt*] into unleashed (*losgelassene*) individuation (*Vereinzelung*)."[116] Unleashed: both unbridled and released from everything, from every commitment and social tie, disseminated. *Vereinzelung*, individuation, singularization, separation: it's an interesting word because, in the code of agriculture (which Heidegger always prefers over that of industry), it means "separation" [*démariage*]. I won't claim that Heidegger thought of this. For German farmers, it is what the French agricultural code refers to as *démariage*, an operation that consists in removing—so as to prevent them from "marrying," precisely, and thus proliferating—a portion of the young plants. Sacrifice and population control in order to maintain an optimal population of the field. In this way, out of demographic concerns, one limits dissemination. *Démariage* also comes down to marriage, to the standardization of

116. Heidegger, "Die Sprache im Gedicht," 46.

births in order to avoid anarchic proliferation. This calculation can be translated into the field of the nation—I'll let you do the math. In the dictionary I consulted, after learning that *Vereinzelung* was the equivalent of *démariage*, I read this conclusion: "The use of precision seeders and monogerm seeds is leading to the disappearance of this practice." One thus no longer needs marriage or *démariage*, it amounts to the same thing once one has precision seeders and monogerm seeds.

In the next sentence, it's no longer just *verschlagen* but also *zerschlagen*, and we find division again:

> Thus divided and scattered (*entzweit und zerschlagen*), the fallen species (*das verfallene Gaschlecht*) is in itself no longer able to find the right strike (*in den rechten Schlag*). [The right strike is reserved for that *Geschlecht* whose twofold, *Zwiefache*, escapes, avoids, gets away from agonistic dissension, *aus der Zwietracht weg*), in accordance with the movement of the stranger, *fram*.] [. . .] It wanders ahead (*vorauswandert*) toward the gentleness [or peace] of a simple twofold, a fold without fold [rather than a "*simplicité dédoublée*" ["split simplicity"], as the French translation has it, *in die Sanftmut einer einfältigen Zwiefalt*].[117]

Simplicity in the two of difference: a strange thing. Unheard of, in the proper sense—the discretion of the inaudible. Strange like the simplicity of a duplicity, the "one-fold" of the "twofold" or the without fold of the fold. But strange, too, because *Geschlecht*, species or sex, moves ahead there, wanders ahead or gets ahead of itself in migration (*vorauswandert*), the path of a journey; and as Heidegger recalled earlier, such is the vocation, such is the sense, then, of *fram, fremd*, the very form of what destines and determines it, its *Bestimmung. Fram, fremd*: that which moves toward an elsewhere, on the way toward what has been reserved in advance.

117. Heidegger, 46.

This is why, after marking this "gentleness of a simple two-fold," Heidegger adds: "that is to say, is a 'strange thing' ('*ein Fremdes*') and thus follows the stranger (*Fremdling*)."[118]

The stranger will be named, at the end of this first part, *der Abgeschiedene*, the one who is departed, the separated one, the dead or deceased one who nevertheless is not dead, the "Dis-ceased" ["*Dis-cédé*"], says the French translation. The peregrination to the right strike follows the path of the Stranger, who is the Other and the Separated One. Going toward him, the soul separates, it becomes the "blue soul," nocturnal and spiritual. It separates itself so as to follow the other over yon, that one, *Jener*. "*Jener*, the poet occasionally says."[119]

Once again, to conclude, we are reminded that: "In the old language (*in der alten Sprache*) *Jener* is pronounced as *ener* and means the 'other' (*der 'andere'*). '*Enert dem Bach*' is the other side of the brook. '*Jener*,' the stranger, is the other for the others, namely, for the decomposing species (*Geschlecht*)."[120] The place of the poem, or rather, of the *Gedicht*, is the departure of the Other, his *Abgeschiedenheit*, which keeps him separated in a place that resembles death, just as his departure resembles a decease, but which is not death. This place has just been pointed at, shown from afar, signified (*angezeigt*) as with a gesture of the finger. A "second step"[121] will have to be clearly remarked.[122]

118. Heidegger, 46.
119. Heidegger, 46.
120. Heidegger, 46.
121. Heidegger, 48.
122. Derrida adds the following note at the very end of the Loyola typescript, addressing those conference participants to whom the text had been distributed: "The transcription of the seminar had to stop here for lack of time. Five sessions, or roughly a hundred pages, remain to be transcribed. Please do not circulate this sketch of a rough draft: *provisional and incomplete*." This thirty-three-page text constitutes the first part of *Geschlecht III*; the remaining pages—the "roughly a hundred pages" or the "five sessions" that "remain to be transcribed"—are drawn from the 1984–85 seminar titled *Philosophical Nationality and Nationalism I: The Ghost of the Other*. See the preface, p. ix.

Ninth Session[1]

Today, then, we are making a start on the second part, we are following what Heidegger calls the "second step" toward this situation of the *Gedicht*, the unspoken place from which all of Trakl's poems are said.

I will not go backwards.

Furthermore, given that this central part, this second of three parts, is the longest and the slowest, with the most winding pathway, today I will not follow the same rhythm as last time (even if this means returning later to moments in the text I will have overstepped), nor the same rhythm, then, nor the same style. I will inevitably have to be more selective, more abrupt, then, and put the text into perspective—which I hope not to do too unfaithfully—so as to clear the possibility of the questions I announced. Regarding the necessity of operating in this way, sometimes patiently following Heidegger's rhythm, keeping step with him, sometimes accelerating, hurrying or rushing things, I explained myself last time.

What, then, will be my questions and thus the criteriology of my choices for this session and this first reading of the second part?

---

1. Here begins the second part of *Geschlecht III*, the "hundred or so pages" that correspond to sessions 9–13 of the 1984–85 seminar.

I could see at least three, three types of questions. Let me very quickly give them provisional titles. The first question will concern what is said about Platonism and Christianity in this interpretation of *Geschlecht* and the two blows, the good and the bad strike. The second will concern, once again, and for reasons I won't go over again because they are the very reason for this seminar, the decisive role that the untranslatable idiom plays in the pathway of this second step. The third question will return to what I announced regarding the one, the unique, the gathering unicity of the *Ort* (the indivisible tip of the spear), a question here made more specific as that of *a difference between polysemy and dissemination.*[2]

Naturally, we won't treat these questions in an entirely dissociated and successive way.

The question of Platonism and Christianity first. It's not the same thing, but Platonism and Christianity are both objects of the same suspicion on Heidegger's part, or the same demarcation. The situation he is attempting is not inscribed or included—no more than the site, the place of Trakl's *Gedicht*—in the Platonic or Christian tradition, despite appearances and signs that might lead us into temptation. In both cases, what is at stake is spirit, the spiritual, the manner of thinking and [reanimating][3] the spiritual, *das Geistliche.*

A.[4] For example, when Trakl "calls the twilight (*Dämmerung*), the night, the years (*Jahre*) of the stranger, his path, '*geistlich*,'"[5] when he says that the dis-cease, *die Abgeschiedenheit*, is spiritual (*geistlich*), he seems to point toward the Christian or ecclesiastical opposition, the one the Church marks between the spiritual and the temporal. But, clearly, Trakl is

---

2. What follow in the typescript of the seminar are four handwritten pages we were able to decipher with the exception of several uncertain words (indicated as such).

3. This word is uncertain in the manuscript.

4. This "A" is not followed by a "B" in the seminar text.

5. Heidegger, "Die Sprache im Gedicht," 54.

not thinking of that spiritualization when he says that oaks are spiritual:

> . . . So geistlich ergrünen
> Die Eichen über den vergessenen Pfaden der Toten,[6]
> . . .
> . . . So spiritual grow verdant
> The oaks over the forgotten paths of the dead,[7]

He is thinking of something more originary, the originarity of "that which has long been dead," an originarity (*Frühe*) promised by "*den 'Frühling der Seele.*'"[8]

So, Trakl does not have Christian spirituality in view, Heidegger concludes very quickly (a bit quickly); but even though this is the case, he could, Heidegger pretends to ask himself, rather than saying *das Geistliche*—which gestures toward this Christian spirituality—have said *geistig*.

> Why does he avoid the word "*geistig*" [and avoid playing with the idiomatic difference between *geistlich* and *geistig*]? [Well, Heidegger responds without hesitating:] Because *geistig* names the opposition [is the *Gegensatz* of] to the material (*Stofflich*). This opposition introduces the distinction between two realms and names, in Western-Platonic language, the abyss between the suprasensuous (*noeton*) from the sensuous (*aistheton*). [Such that, on the basis of this opposition between *noeton* and *aistheton*,] the *geistig* thus understood, which has meanwhile become the rational, intellectual, and ideological, belongs, along with its oppositions, to the worldview of *des verwesenden Geschlechtes* [of the decomposing species/sex].[9]

6. Trakl, "In Hellbrunn," quoted in Heidegger, "Die Sprache im Gedicht," 54.
7. Trakl, "In Hellbrunn," in *Poems and Prose*, 111.
8. Heidegger, "Die Sprache im Gedicht," 55.
9. Heidegger, 55.

Now, the *Abgeschiedenheit* Trakl speaks of is *geistlich* and not *geistig*; Trakl names it in a non-metaphysical, non-Platonic, and non-Christian way. Spirit, *Geist*, according to Trakl, according to his last poem, *Grodek*, is what *burns*: "In his last poem, 'Grodek,' Trakl speaks of the '*heißen Flamme des Geistes*.' Spirit is that which flames and only as such is it perhaps that which wafts. Trakl understands spirit not primarily as *pneuma*, or as *spiritus* [another demarcation], but as flame, which enflames, rouses, transports [*entsetzt*, moves outside], and brings into disorder (*außer Fassung bringt*). Flame is a glowing luminescence."[10] Once again, here's the idiom coming to the aid of interpretation, "*in der ursprünglichen Bedeutung des Wortes*," *Geist* means this, "because *gheis* signifies: to be upset, transported, outside oneself "[11] (see Hegel and *Glas*[12]).

Such that, at the very moment when Trakl situated by Heidegger seems, as one often says, as close as can be to a Christian thinking, he says *something else*. He doesn't say the opposite, he says something that is more *originary*—this distinction is what my question will be about in a moment.

He is even closer to a Christian thinking (and here we will rediscover the theme of the curse (*Fluch*) from last week) given that "spirit thus understood essences in the [double] possibility of both the gentle [gathering, peace, tenderness] *and* the destructive (*Zerstörerischen*)."[13] Evil—and this time Heidegger names Evil as such (*das Böse*)—also comes from spirit. "Evil and its wickedness (*Bosheit*) are not the sensuous, the material. Evil is not of a merely spiritual nature either [beyond opposition, it is not '*geistig*,' it is '*geistlich*,' the frightening, dispersing, *Ungesammelte*, unholy, non-salvation, *Unheilen*, etc.]."[14] There is a valence of *Geist* that Heidegger does not put to work in this entire *Erörterung*, namely, that of ghost

10. Heidegger, 56.
11. Heidegger, 56.
12. See Derrida, *Glas*.
13. Heidegger, "Die Sprache im Gedicht," 56.
14. Heidegger, 56.

or *revenant*, which nevertheless would seem to impose itself and be motivated by the entire context. We might ask why.

In any case, according to him:

> To the extent that the essence of *Geist* lies in enflaming (*Entflammen*), it breaks the way (*bricht er Bahn*), illuminates it, and sets on a path [that which is *fremd, fram*]. As flame, spirit is the storm that "launches an attack on the heavens," "on a quest for God," and casts the soul on the way [the soul that is a strange thing on earth]. [. . .] It is spirit which gives the soul as a gift. It is the *Beseeler* [the animator, the soul in turn maintains spirit by nourishing it].[15]

There is nothing here that is anti-Christian, nor a-Christian, nor even a- or anti-Platonic. Heidegger would say: it is more originary than Platonism and Christianity.[16] It is that which allows, it is a more originary structure and language on the basis of which Platonism and Christianity, as forms of decomposition, are possible and thinkable, derived. But what does this repetition do, then, if it says nothing, does nothing other than implicitly repeat, at a more originary level, the *same content* that it would only *double* with its ghost, as it were?

(One can very well imagine a Christian—Kant, for example, or Hegel, if one thinks of his logic but also his theology—recognizing and accepting this derivation as the proper situation of Christianity. In short, Heidegger proposes no other *content*, only an originary, pre-originary double *on the basis of which* Platonism and Christianity could be produced, as decomposed forms. The *geistlich/geistig* difference is that of a repetition doubling the same . . .)

That's the *first question*, but you see that I dealt with it by passing through the second, that of the idiom. We will now

---

15. Heidegger, 56–57. This quotation is followed by an illegible word in parentheses.

16. Crossed-out words: "But what does this repetition do, then?"

deal with it again by passing through the third question, that of polysemy and dissemination.[17]

This question of polysemy (this is not Heidegger's word) of course has an essential link to the question of duality and repetition that we are constantly talking about. To hear this link, we will once again cross paths with the absolute idiom. Let's start back up from dis-cease, *Abgeschiedenheit*, as the place of Trakl's *Gedicht*. "The dis-ceased, we call them the dead."[18] But what death is this? "Into what death has the stranger died?"[19]

The answer comes from another poem, which says:

> Der Wahnsinnige ist gestorben.[20]
> . . .
> The madman is dead.[21]

From there—in accordance with the metonymic sliding from one poem to another that we have already talked about, from a given line in a given poem responding to another line in another poem—we pass first to the following stanza, which says "*Man begräbt den Fremden* (The stranger is buried)," then to another line from another poem, "Siebengesang des Todes," which speaks of the "white stranger";[22] we have passed, then, from a dead man in one poem, to a buried stranger in another, to a "white stranger" in a third, and, finally, a fourth metonymy in another poem, "Psalm": "In his grave plays the white magician with his snakes" (*In seinem Grab spielt der weiße Magier mit seinen Schlangen*)."[23] If he is playing, we can say (and Hei-

---

17. The typed text of the seminar resumes here.

18. Heidegger, 48.

19. Heidegger, 48.

20. Trakl, "Psalm," quoted in Heidegger, "Die Sprache im Gedicht," 49.

21. Trakl, "Psalm I," in *Poems and Prose*, 18/19.

22. Trakl, "Siebengesang des Todes," quoted in Heidegger, "Die Sprache im Gedicht," 49; "Sevenfold Song of Death," in *Poems and Prose*, 87/86.

23. Trakl, "Psalm," quoted in Heidegger, 49; "Psalm I," in *Poems and Prose*, 18/19.

degger does not fail to do so) that the dead man is alive in his grave. And this living dead man is—back to square one, going back up the chain of metonymies—this living white strange dead man is the Madman: *der Wahnsinnige*. "But does madman mean mentally ill? Not at all."[24] And here, once again, the untranslatable idiom comes up. "*Wahnsinn* (madness) *bedeutet nicht* (does not signify) the musings [meditation or dreaming, *Sinnen*] that the madman fancies [imagines, wrongly believes, *wähnt*]," it is not the fancy that the crazy person fixes on. This is not how we should hear the word "*Wahnsinn*." Once again, we must go back to Old High German: *wana* signifies "without" (*ohne*). What will Heidegger do with this "without"? Here the sentence is untranslatable: "*Der Wahnsinnige sinnt* [the madman muses—a rupture in the idiomatic family; this can only be said in German]," he muses but if *der Wahnsinnige sinnt* this is because he has sense, the madman is within sense, he is not lacking in *Sinn*, and he even "*sinnt* (he muses, a trivial sense of *sinnt*) [. . .] as no other does (*wie keiner sonst*)."[25] One can intimate (more and better than others). But what is to be done then with the *ohne* (without)<?>. "The madman (*Wahnsinnige*) remains without the sense of others (*er bleibt dabei ohne den Sinn der Anderen*)," which is translated incorrectly, excessively, and a bit ridiculously as "but in that he went back on what sense is for others."[26] Same for the translation of the next sentence: "he is otherwise sensed" for "*Er ist anderen Sinnes*": "he is of another sense."[27] Which means that he separates himself from others with respect to sense, he does not have or does not make the same sense as others, but he is not deprived of sense, he is not without sense, he is without others, if you prefer, without the sense of others. But what does sense mean then, what is the sense of sense, and of

24. Heidegger, "Die Sprache im Gedicht," 49.
25. Heidegger, 49.
26. Heidegger, 49. The French translation reads: "mais il s'est dédit en cela de ce qui est sens pour les autres."
27. Heidegger, 49. The French translation reads: "il est autrement sensé."

Sinn, sinnen<?>. Here the recourse to the High German idiom is not simply one more recourse among others, it is even more decisive because it is a question of the sense of the word "sense." If the word "sense" is an idiom, once we recognize that like every idiom it entails untranslatability, then it is the very concept of translation—and thus of idiom—that becomes problematic because it is based on at least some implicit consensus as to sense and as to the sense of the word "sense," as to the translatability of sense and of the sense of sense. Now, not only is the word "*sinnan*," in the originary value that Heidegger wants to resituate or restore to it, untranslatable, but its "sense" has an essential affinity, as you will see, with this word "*fram*," the stranger that could only say what it says in German and whose originary sense orients the entire "situation" (*Erörterung*). We asked ourselves what consequences were to be drawn from the fact that a word that signifies stranger for us does not really signify stranger (*extraneus*) and has a sense that can resonate only within the boundaries of one language. If we are able to translate it, as we are nevertheless going to translate *sinnan*, this is because Heidegger's *Erörterung*, even as it sticks to or returns to a place of origin, already carries out a translation within German, of Germans of different ages, different generations (Old High German, Modern German, philosophical code, everyday code, etc.). Heidegger already carries out a sort of translative, Germano-German back-and-forth. And it is this back-and-forth, its explication in Modern or everyday German of what the Old High German meant that allows us to translate into French and to speak as I am doing. It is because Heidegger engages in this translation toward or from the originary sense of sense that Germans, for starters, can read it, supposing they do read it (and you know that many Germans don't want to or can't read it, snickering at these French people who take these extravagances of writing seriously). So what does *sinnan* mean? "'*Sinnan*' bedeutet *ursprünglich* (signifies originarily) *reisen, streben nach* . . . (to travel, to strive for . . . [ellipsis])," and Heidegger adds one more synonym, "*eine Richtung einschlagen*," "*prendre une direction*" ["to take a direction"] says the French translation, which loses the *schlagen* along the way: *eine Richtung einschlagen* is to open in one blow [*d'un coup*] or to imprint a direction (*einschlagen* has many senses depending on the context and the many typical or idiomatic phrases in which it is used, but you always find this force of the blow through which one embarks or sets out, it is also used in constructions with *Weg, den Weg, den falschen Weg einschlagen*: to take the wrong path, to set out on the wrong path with the movement of a decision, in one blow one sets out this way rather than that way).[28] So, *sinnan* is *eine Richtung einschlagen*: to strike out in a direction, in a direction [*sens*] in the sense of a path. And Heidegger specifies right away that the Indo-European root *sent* and *set* means *Weg* (path). "The dis-ceased is the madman (*Wahnsinnige*) because he is on the way toward elsewhere (*er anderswohin unterwegs ist*)," without the sense of others.[29] The madman is on the way (*unterwegs*) toward elsewhere. Let us not say in Latin or in French that he is *extravagant*. He is not extra(-) because *fram* or *ohne* or *sinnen* and without do not want to relate to the alienness [*extranéité*] of the stranger, but also because he does not roam, he does not vagabond, he does not err, he doesn't go just anywhere, as we noted. He has a destination.

Here I am opening a long parenthesis; I call it a "parenthesis" a bit unfairly, let's say an excursus but certainly not a parenthesis if one puts in parentheses something secondary or inessential to the matter at hand. In truth, I am putting in this excursus the thing that interests me the most, perhaps, in the reading of this text. What is Heidegger doing? What movement, what path, what madness, what sense or other sense is he describing, what or whom is he speaking of in this

28. We close the parenthesis here.
29. Heidegger, "Die Sprache im Gedicht," 49.

supposed situation of Trakl's *Gedicht*<?> Take a good look. He is speaking, I won't say of himself, Martin Heidegger, but certainly of his own approach. Heidegger reads and writes here, in the footsteps [*sur la trace*] of Trakl's place, like someone that literary or poetic critics, or philologists, or philosophers, men of knowledge, would judge to be mad; he seems to err, to jump from one poem to another, he peregrinates, alone, a stranger, or in the footsteps of another, he is at once the dead man and the stranger, he is playing in his grave, and so on. He speaks of himself, then, when speaking of the other, he speaks of his place when speaking of the place of the other, or, rather, he is in search of his place when following the steps of the other, and so forth. However, and one can also pursue this analysis in this direction—I mean the analysis of a Heidegger text that is in short only the signature or stamp or blow of Heidegger—one can pursue this by saying, as he himself says of the stranger (*fram*, *fremd*), that he is on the move, on the way, peregrinating, but that (and here my question to come about determination announces itself), his path has a destination (a *Bestimmung*), as he himself said of the stranger on the way (*fram*), he is not going just anywhere, he is not reading and writing in just any way, he is not erring when he jumps from one poem to another or from one line to another. I won't say that he knows where he's going, for this destination, this determination in the destination, this *Bestimmung*, is not of the order of knowledge, but still, he has an orientation and a path (*sent*, *set*), a *Sinn* that pre-orients, magnetizes, and draws along his approach, and his conversation with Trakl. He is not going just anywhere in the Trakl text. Incidentally, this is exactly what so-called competent people (philosophers, philologists, poetic critics) criticize him for; they criticize him both for saying whatever, arbitrarily, without taking account of the internal organization or the apparent meaning of the text, and for not saying whatever, and imposing on Trakl a situation and a place pre-determined by

Heidegger, and for making the poet say, from this place, what he wants to say or hear him say. In any case, whatever one makes of it, one cannot overlook—and this is what I wanted to mark in this excursus—this situation of Heidegger himself, and this scene according to which he speaks of himself or, rather, of his proper place, his own step, his own pathway, in short, his signature. And this is not a criticism in my view. It is no doubt the condition of every situation. In a moment, I will formulate a question from this point of view that will be less confident, let's say . . . I close the parenthesis.

We are continuing to follow this pathway, marking stations by places where the idiom plays a role that is determining, or destining, precisely. Because the madman is on the way toward elsewhere, his madness can be called "gentle" (*sanft*, tender, etc.).[30] This gentleness, as the gentleness of the stranger, serves as a metonymic transition toward another poem that will considerably enrich the space of meditation and will allow us to take up again the thinking of *Geschlecht*. This poem, titled "To One Who Died Young" ("An einen Frühverstorbenen," to one who died too early) speaks of the stranger by calling him "*Jener*" (the other, as Heidegger reminded us).[31] This stranger has a "blue smile" on his face and he was, I'm quoting the French translation, "strangely taken up by the chrysalis of his childhood, a more serene peace, and then died (*und seltsam verpuppt, in seine stillere Kindheit und starb*)."[32] Death of the child entering his morning or taken up by *die Frühe*, and which Heidegger puts in proximity, still by way of metonymy, with an adolescent (*Knabe*, a young boy) in another poem, "Am Mönchsberg" ("By the Mönchsberg"). This

30. Heidegger, 49.
31. Trakl, "An einen Frühverstorbenen," quoted in Heidegger, 49; "To One Who Died Young," in *Poems and Prose*, 74/75.
32. Trakl, in Heidegger, 49; "To One Who Died Young," in *Poems and Prose*, 74/75.

one who died young is the figure of Elis, which the poet addresses in the following way:

> O wie lange bist, Elis, du verstorben. [33]
> . . .
> O how long, Elis, have you been dead.[34]

Elis, says Heidegger, "is the stranger called into decline (*in den Untergang gerufene Fremdling*)."[35] And he clarifies immediately—which will allow us to clarify what I was suggesting a moment ago when I was saying that Heidegger speaks to us of his own path—Heidegger clarifies immediately:

> Elis is in no way a figure through which Trakl refers to himself (*sich selber meint*). Elis is as essentially distinct from the poet as the thinker Nietzsche is from Zarathustra. [But this comparison is not made randomly.] Both figures, however, have in common the fact that their essence and wandering (*Wesen und Wandern*) begin with decline [comment on Zarathustra, descent from the mountain, and so on].[36]

This allows me to clarify, then, that when I was saying that Heidegger speaks, in sum, whether he meant to or not, of himself and his signature, I did not mean this in the conventionally autobiographical sense that Heidegger here rejects with regard to the relation between Elis and Trakl. But I will persist in saying, in another register, according to another regime, that Heidegger is speaking of himself (to be understood otherwise than in accordance with psychology, subjectivity and the ego), of his place and what occurs with him in his approach and his signature, just as I would say that Nietzsche speaks of

33. Trakl, "An den Knaben Elis," quoted in Heidegger, 53.
34. Trakl, "To the Boy Elis," in *Poems and Prose*, 42/43.
35. Heidegger, "Die Sprache im Gedicht," 50.
36. Heidegger, 50.

himself in this sense in Zarathustra and that Trakl speaks of himself under the name Elis. It remains to be seen what speaking of oneself means. I close the parenthesis again.

> The decline of Elis goes toward the ancient morning [*Frühe, uralte Frühe*, the arche-originary dawn] that is more ancient than the old decomposing *Geschlecht* (*älter ist denn das altgewordene verwesende Geschlecht*), more ancient because it is more pensive [*sinnender*: recall what was just said of *sinnen*], more *sinnend* because it is more still (*stiller*), more still because it is itself more soothing (*stillender*).[37]

Elis would name, then, a more ancient and more peaceful place than the old *Geschlecht* (old species or old sex) that received the bad blow, the second blow of the curse that introduced the two of discord, sexual difference as discord. And it is indeed a question of sexual difference, of *Geschlecht* as sex, as well, and not only as species, as the French translation translates it, missing here an essential determination of this passage. Elis goes toward a sexuality, if you will, more ancient than that of the old sex that is torn apart by sexual difference of an agonistic and oppositional type. And, in fact, what does Heidegger go on to say just after? Well, that:

> In the figure of the boy Elis, *das Knabenhafte* (the being of the boy) does not lie in an opposition (*in einem Gegensatz*) to the being of the girl (*zum Mädchenhaften*). *Das Knabenhafte ist die Erscheinung der stilleren Kindheit* [which is strangely translated into French as "the boy Elis is the apparition of profound childhood" ["*le garçon Elis est l'apparition de l'enfance profonde*"] whereas the text says: the being-boy (*das Knabenhafte*, naturally, implied, that of Elis) is the phenomenon or the appearing (*Erscheinung*) of a childhood that is more peaceful (silent, soothing, etc.,

37. Heidegger, 50–51.

that childhood in which boy and girl are not opposed)].
The latter shelters and keeps in itself *die sanfte Zwiefalt der Geschlechter* [the gentle division, the gentle or tender duality of the sexes, thus a sexual difference, a two that is not yet determined and unleashed into opposition, the adolescent boy and the adolescent girl alike], of the *Jüngling* as well as of "the golden figure of the girl" (*der "goldenen Gestalt der Jünglingin"*).[38]

Elis is not a dead one who comes undone (*verwest*), who decomposes in the manner of the decomposing *Geschlecht*. He is the dead who "*entwest*" (not translated), difficult to translate, Heidegger displaces the everyday meaning, which is "to destroy," or even "to disinfest," toward that of to "dis-essence," as it were, to unfold one's *Wesen* backwards, toward "*die Frühe*": who dis-essences, or dis-essences himself toward the morning, or the arche-origin. "This stranger unfolds the human essence (*entfaltet das Menschenwesen*) in advance [ahead, *voraus*] toward the beginning [or departure, *Anbeginn*] of that which has not yet been carried out [*n'est pas encore advenu à portée*] (*noch nicht zum Tragen gekommen*)."[39] The French word *porter* ["to carry," "to bear"], *tragen* here, of course has the sense of producing, of bearing in the sense of production, but you will see this word communicate (something the French translation misses entirely), on the one hand, with *austragen*, which means to bear in the sense of to carry a child before its birth and up to its birth (*ein ausgetragenes Kind* is a child born at term, carried to term) and, on the other hand, with a word that belongs to the Heideggerian idiom, by which I mean a word that Heidegger appropriated to what he says of difference, in particular in the text that precedes this one in *Unterwegs zur Sprache*, "*Die Sprache*," where the words "*Austrag*" and "*austragen*" come to say something essential about

38. Heidegger, 51.
39. Heidegger, 51.

Unter-Schied (difference): "The intimacy of dif-ference is the unifying element of *diaphora*, of a carrying to term that carries through."[40] The figure or process of being carried to term (as one says of the child), the figure of bearing as dif-ference is *Austrag*, which becomes a kind of synonym of difference in Heidegger's text (I refer you to these other passages for the moment). Here Elis, the dead stranger, "unfolds the human essence in advance toward what has not yet been carried to term [what has not yet been borne, *noch nicht zum Tragen . . . gekommen*]."[41] And Heidegger adds in parentheses "Old High German *giberan*," so, that which is not yet born (unborn,[42] *Ungeborene*). And this word, "*Ungeborene*," is Trakl's. "The poet [says Heidegger] calls the quieter and thus more soothing *Unausgetragene* [not carried to term, and not '*inexporté*' ['unexported'] as the French translation has it, and thus also undifferentiated] in the essence of mortals *das Ungeborene* ['*l'ingénéré*' ['the ungenerated'] says the French translation]."[43]

And Heidegger quotes another line, another poem, "Heiterer Früling" ("Bright Springtime"):

> Und Ungebornes pflegt der eignen Ruh.
> . . .
> And the unborn cultivates over his own repose.

The unborn tends to and preserves (*wahrt*) the more soothing childhood into the coming awakening to come of the *Menschengeschlechtes* [of the human race—or the sex to come]. Thus, in repose, the one who died young *lives*. [. . .] The departed gazes ahead into the blue of spiritual night. The white eyelids, which protect his gaze, shine in the nuptial [rather, bridal] jewelry that promises [*verspricht*, all of this is

40. Heidegger, "Die Sprache," 22.
41. Heidegger, "Die Sprache im Gedicht," 51.
42. In English in the original. (—Trans.)
43. Heidegger, 51.

a meditation on the promise, and we should—and perhaps we will later—take an interest in it from this perspective] *die sanftere Zwiefalt des Geschlecht* ["the more gentle division of *genre* ["genus," "gender"]," says the French translation, of sex, too, that promises a sexual difference without discord].[44]

I must deal by preterition with a meditation on gold in Trakl's poems, gold that is in tune with this gentle madness, this childhood of the unborn, this departure (*Anbeginn*) that is also a "dark patience of the end":

> Goldenes Auge des Anbeginns, dunkle Geduld des Endes.[45]

This end, the end *des verwesenden Geschlechtes* (of the corrupt species or sex—a Christian word, but . . .) does not come after the beginning. "The end, as end of the corrupted *Geschlecht* [or in corruption], precedes the beginning of the ungenerated sex."[46] This ungeneration of *Geschlecht* remains to come, then, and it is what is awaited, what the golden gaze foresees: the dark patience of the end. But in order for the end to precede the beginning, in order to think this, we must free ourselves of the Aristotelian concept of time that has dominated all of Western metaphyiscs[47] (see "*Ousia* and *Gramme*":[48] linearity as well as circularity, including Hegel, etc.).

It is not only the treatment of gold that I must pass over for the moment, but also that of stone, of the stone that speaks,

---

44. Heidegger, 51. The French translation here reads: "le plus tendre dédoublement du genre." In the typescript, this is followed by a handwritten note: "gold—stone—descendants [*neveux*]—[one or two illegible words]—75."

45. Trakl, "Jahr," quoted in Heidegger, "Die Sprache im Gedicht," 53; "Year," in *Poems and Prose*, 94/95.

46. Heidegger, 53.

47. Heidegger, 53.

48. Derrida, "*Ousia* and *Gramme*: Note on a Note from *Being and Time*," in *Margins of Philosophy*, 29–68.

in order to more quickly reach this question that I announced concerning polysemy and dissemination.

If I use the word dissemination, I do so not in order to re-center things toward a certain word I privileged in the past, a word which has to do with anything but recentering. I do so in order better to bring out a relation, one I believe to be necessary, between the scene of *Geschlecht* as a scene both sexual and genealogical, of engendering and generation on the one hand, and the more narrowly linguistic question sheltered in the impossible couple I call dissemination/polysemy.

Skipping over the passage on evil and *geistlich* that I jumped ahead and spoke of a moment ago, I pick up the course of the text at the place where, underscoring that "the hymn (the *Gesang*) is *Lied* (song), tragedy and *epos* all in one," and that the *Dichtung*, the spoken poetry[49] of Trakl, is unique (*einzig*) because in it everything gathers itself in "the simplicity of saying (*das Einfache des Sagens*) in an unsayable manner (*auf eine unsägliche Weise*)," Heidegger comes back to this affirmation according to which evil, or rather "pain (*Schmerz*) is only truly pain when it serves the flame of spirit."[50] And he then cites Trakl's final poem, which in general is celebrated as a war poem, and which Heidegger says is something more and other than that. "The final lines of the poem say":[51]

> The ardent flame of spirit, today a mighty pain nourishes it
> The ungenerated descendants (*Die ungebornen Enkel*).[52]

---

49. At first glance, Heidegger's text seems to suggest that it is rather (or also) a question here of Trakl's poem "Verklärung" ("Transfiguration")—and not of his spoken poetry in general—a poem "unique among all" (*einzig unter allen*) insofar as it is "song, tragedy, and *epos* all in one." Heidegger, "Die Sprache im Gedicht," 61.

50. Heidegger, 61.

51. Heidegger, 61.

52. Trakl, "Grodek," quoted in Heidegger, 61; "Grodek," in *Poems and Prose*, 126/127.

Enkel means descendants in general, but from the sense of the French word *neveux*, which in Latin (*nepos*), as in French, first means grandsons before it signifies "nephews" in the modern sense. When Descartes speaks of his *neveux* (somewhere or other) he is speaking of the generations to come.[53] Here Heidegger takes an interest in this word *Enkel*, noting that "the descendants are not the ungenerated sons of the sons fallen in war [the usual reading of the poem]," they do not name in the poem "the interruption of the propagation of the generations (*Geschlechter*) up until now," because in that case, given that the species is undergoing corruption, "the poet should rather rejoice," at least within the logic that Heidegger attributes to him.[54] For Heidegger, it's a question of a "*'stolzere Trauer'* [quotation]," a mourning that is higher, more elevated, prouder, haughtier, and which:

> [. . .] flaming, beholds the repose of the unborn (*die Ruhe des Ungeborenen*). The unborn [the unbegotten] are called "descendants" because they cannot be sons, that is, the immediate [or direct] offspring of the *verfallenen Geschlecht* [of the fallen species or sex]. Between them and this species [or this *Geschlecht*] lives another generation ["*Generation*" this time]. This generation is other because it is of another kind, in accordance with its other essential provenance from the morning [the origin] of the unborn.[55]

Thus, the dis-cease (*Abgeschiedenheit*), the departure, of the separation of the dead man, of the one who died too young (Elis), is the spirit in its flame insofar as it gathers, <insofar as> it is "that which gathers" and that which, gathering,

---

53. Interlinear addition: "Descendants [*Neveux*]: skipped generation . . ."
54. Heidegger, "Die Sprache im Gedicht," 62.
55. Heidegger, 62.

[. . .] retrieves the essence of mortals into its more soothing childhood, shelters it [in its breast] as (*als*) *den nicht ausgetragene Schlag* [the stamp or blow not yet carried to term] which stamps (*prägt*) the *Geschlecht* to come (*das künftige Geschlecht*). [And I emphasize what resembles, once again and not fortuitously, a Christian vocabulary; Heidegger speaks here of resurrection, *Auferstehung*: only meaning of the word, "resurrection." He says that:] That which gathers in dis-cease [the gathering of *Abgeschiedenheit*] keeps [protects, spares, *spart*] the unborn, beyond the dead [in the everyday sense, *Abgelebte*], toward [in anticipation of, *hinweg in*, on the way toward] a coming resurrection of human kind (*Menschenschlages*) from out of [starting from] the morning (*aus der Frühe*). [This gathering of the one who died young or of the unborn prepares the resurrection to come of the *Geschlecht*.] As the spirit of the gentle, that which gathers likewise soothes the spirit of evil [that is, of this malignity that reaches its apogee in the *Zwietracht* of the sexes that comes to break, burst in, all the way into the *Geschwisterliche*, into the relation between brother and sister].[56]

Sexual discord, sexual difference as *Zwietracht*, as agonistic duality, is thus that which perturbs a serene sexual difference, the one that supposedly takes place between brother and sister before the curse and before evil, the bad flame of spirit. This *Geschwisterliche*, this relation between brother and sister, would not be asexual, then, but a sexual relation in a difference without dissension. I will let you read, following this passage, this whole scene of brother/sister. And I come, then—you see why now, and why I spoke of dissemination—to the linguistic form, as it were, of this problem. Further on, indeed, quoting a line that says "*die Schönheit eines heimkehrenden Geschlechts*

56. Heidegger, 62.

[the splendor, the beauty of a species or sex that has come back, that returns home],"[57] Heidegger underscores the necessity, in order to understand the saying of this poetry, not to "stop at the dull [stultified, obtuse: *stumpf*, having no point, flat!] sense of a univocal meaning [*vouloir dire*]."[58] The sense is *stumpf* (dull, obtuse) if it is that of an "*eindeutigen Meinens*," of a single intention of saying, a one-way intention. We must hear the plurivocity, the *Mehrdeutigkeit*. Heidegger recalls that each of the words he more or less read, "twilight and night, decline and death, madness and game, pond and rock, bird flight and boat, stranger and brother, spirit and God, as well as the words for colors: blue and green, white and black, red and silver, golden and dark, [all of these] each time say the multiple [the fold of the multiple, *Mehrfältiges*]."[59] He gives examples of this and follows up by noting that what one calls *Mehrdeutige* (I am translating this as "polysemy," the more than one meaning, the many meanings) is itself "at first glance ambiguous (*zweideutig*)."[60] In other words, there are two ways of thinking or determining polysemy, *Mehrdeutigkeit*.

> But this ambiguity [this duplicity of the double meaning, *Zweideutigkeit*] itself, as a whole, comes to stand again on one side, the other side of which is determined on the basis of the most inner place (*Ort*) of the *Gedicht* [unspoken; such that the] poetry (*Dichtung*) speaks on the basis of an ambiguous ambiguity [a duplicity of meaning that is itself duplicitous (*aus einer zweideutigen Zweideutigkeit*)].[61]

Ambiguity is ambiguous, the two of meaning is double, twice two, meaning is twice double, double in a double sense.

57. Trakl, "Offenbarung und Untergang," quoted in Heidegger, 70; "Revelation and Perdition," in *Poems and Prose*, 126/127.
58. Heidegger, 71.
59. Heidegger, 71.
60. Heidegger, 71.
61. Heidegger, 71.

And this is where the question that I call the question of dissemination comes in.

> However, this polysemy of the poetic saying [*dieses Mehr-deutige* of the poetic saying, says Heidegger, and this is essential to what he is saying for the reasons with which I began this reading], this plurality of meaning of the poetic saying does not scatter into indeterminate equivocality [does not disseminate, does not become scattered in the wind here and there with an indeterminate polyvalence, *flattert nicht ins unbestimmte Vieldeutige auseinander*].[62]

It gathers itself. Plurality gathers itself, the polysemy converges, and it is on this condition that there is a poetic place, a *Gedicht*, that is, this *Ort*, this tip of the spear toward which all tensions tend to meet. It is even from this gathering that the plurality of poetic tones takes its source and comes to harmonize in a unique resonance (*Einklang*). Heidegger writes:

> *Der mehrdeutige Ton* (the tone with multiple meanings) of Trakl's *Gedicht* comes from out of a gathering (*Versammlung*), i.e. (*d.h.*), from out of a unison [a harmony, *Einklang*, insofar as it belongs to the *Gedicht*, which is always unspoken, unsaid, this unison, this *Einklang* that must be heard] that remains for its part always unspeakable (*stets unsäglich bleibt*). The polysemy (*Mehrdeutige*) of this poetic saying is not [said with a sort of clear contempt] *das Ungenaue des Lässigen* [the imprecision, inexactness, vagueness, and not the "*relâchement*" ["slackening"], as the French translation has it, of laisser-aller, of nonchalance, carefreeness], but rather the rigor (*die Strenge*) of a letting-be [Heidegger opposes letting go, *Lässingen*, to letting-be, *Lassenden*] that has let itself engage (*eingelassen*) with the care [the scrupulousness, *Sorgfalt*] of "*gerechten Anschauen*"

62. Heidegger, 71.

[a quote, of the correct view] and that complies to it [joins or adjusts itself to it].[63]

With a gesture that I, for my part, find very classical or even Aristotelian (I'll say why in a moment), Heidegger does not imagine any alternative other than that of a polysemy that is gathered or that gathers in the unity of the tone of the *Gedicht*—a poetry of rigor—and, on the other hand, a dispersion that is careless, vague, in short, without place, a dispersion of the indeterminacy of the whatever, of the irreducible multiplicity of tones and meaning which, for Heidegger, can only fall under *laisser-aller*. There can be no rigorous thinking or poetic writing of dissemination. Heidegger will push on in that direction in the following paragraph, but before we get there, why did I say that this was traditional and Aristotelian first of all (even though one can, in the wake of Aristotle, cite numerous other representatives in this same vein which has been and remains dominant not only in philosophy but everywhere, in particular in hermeneutics and poetics)?[64] It is because, for Aristotle, polysemy is acceptable; a word—and thus everything that can be done with words (sentences, texts)—can have multiple meanings, on the condition that this plurality is ordered and unifiable, that it has, *qua* plurality of meaning, a focal meaning. Otherwise, says Aristotle (for example, in the *Metaphysics*, Gamma 1006 a30-b15), "for not to have one meaning is to have no meaning" (*to gar mē hen sēmainein outhen sēmainein estin*).[65] Even if one follows this very strong and still dominant logic, it would remain to be seen whether the language or the text (the mark, and in particular the so-called poetic mark, the one that issues from a *Gedicht*) is still, must still be of the order of signification (*Bedeutung* or *semainein*).

63. Heidegger, 71.
64. We close the parenthesis.
65. Aristotle, *The Complete Works of Aristotle*, The Revised Oxford Translation, ed. Jonathan Barnes (Princeton, NJ: Princeton University Press, 1995), 2:1589.

In any case, for Heidegger there is no question that there is poetic saying only if the polyphony is gathered in a *Grundton* (even if this *Grundton* is, like the *Gedicht*, inaudible), and only if this *Grundton* takes its source in one unique and gathering place. No irreducible difference, difference itself must be, as he says elsewhere, unified, carried to term, it is one as such, it is unique (see the previous text, "Die Sprache").⁶⁶

Emphasizing evaluation and hierarchization with an increasing severity (in a nutshell, good polysemy, bad dissemination), Heidegger recognizes that the limit between these two is difficult to recognize, as is the case with the border between the great poet who, you will remember, devotes himself to the unicity of his place and others who, in short, have no proper place, do not take place and are doomed to disseminal errancy.

> Often, we can hardly distinguish [demarcate the boundary, *abgrenzen*, that separates] the polysemic saying [. . .] that properly belongs (*eignet*) to Trakl's poems from the language of other poets, the equivocality (*Vieldeutigkeit*) of which stems from [descends, comes from, is born of, *stammt aus*] the indeterminacy [*Unbestimmten*: so, from the absence of determination and destination, of *Bestimmung*], of the indetermination of an insecurity [*Unsicherheit*: now Heidegger disqualifies insecurity] of a poetical groping around (*des poetischen Umhertastens*).⁶⁷

Heidegger does not say why the boundary is difficult to trace nor, especially, how one may recognize it. He does not say why both of these (gatherable polysemy and irreducible dissemination) resemble one another and split apart, why the place and the non-place resemble one another and split apart, why one of them does not accidentally reach the other, etc. He affirms only that there is place, that there is the place and therefore the

---

66. Heidegger, "Die Sprache," 25.
67. Heidegger, "Die Sprache im Gedicht," 71.

boundary, and that, beyond or on this side of dissemination, nomadization, or groping around (a pejorative term for errancy without homeland), there is an *Ort*, a homeland, a *Gedicht*, and ultimately an absolute univocity of language. But since he has just said that there is plurivocity, a good plurivocity in Trakl, and that, moreover, he always placed exactitude, security, *Sicherheit*, univocity on the side of Cartesian metaphysics, technics, and science, he will now have to distinguish between two univocities, the good one and the bad one, the high one and the low one. The "high one" and the "low one," yes indeed: that of the poem, the high one of the great poet, and that of science, the low one. Let me read:

> The unique rigor of Trakl's essentially plurivocal language (*die einzigartige Strenge der wesenhaft mehrdeutigen Sprache Trakls*) is in a higher sense (*in einem höheren Sinne*) so univocal (*so eindeutig*) that it remains infinitely (*unendlich*) superior even to all the technical exactitude [*Exaktheit*, in Husserl *streng, exakt*] of the merely scientific-univocal concept (*des bloß wissenschaftlich-eindeutigen Begriffes*).[68]

One ends up in a situation where the unique univocity that gathers poetic plurivocity (as *Ort*, the tip of the spear gathers the multiplicity of tensions to the highest degree), this unicity of poetic univocity is superior, higher than both dissemination or irreducible polytonality and scientific univocity, as the ideal of scientificity. Dissemination winds up paradoxically on the same side, that is, beneath, on the same side as science, technics, and ultimately metaphysics (security, assurance, etc.). It is this strange situation and this combination that interest me. We will come back to this next week.

68. Heidegger, 71.

Tenth Session

Let me recall briefly the three questions the threads of which I crossed or tied in a knot, as it were, two weeks ago. The first question, which we will return to again today, concerned what is said about Platonism and Christianity in this interpretation of *Geschlecht* and of the two blows (the good and the bad), as well as in this interpretation or situation of Trakl's *Gedicht* itself. The second question dealt with the regular occurrence of idiomatic and fundamentally untranslatable expressions, with the recourse to Old German, of which we saw and analyzed several examples. This second question was revived last week with a question from Hachem Foda[1] on the unspoken character of the *Gedicht*. I clarified then that even though the *Gedicht* remains, according to Heidegger, unspoken (*ungesprochen*), it was not, as the source of the *Dichtungen*, *something other* than the written or spoken—in truth, sung—poems. It is their originary place, the place of their source and also, then, of their gathering, the place from which they proceed and toward which, in accordance with the *rhuthmos*, their course flows back. There are not two things, the *Gedicht* and the *Dichtungen*; the silence of the former already belongs to the pronouncement of the latter or, if you prefer, the other way around. What's more, the *Grundton* that Heidegger read, as you recall perhaps, in the word "*Ein*" of

1. Here and on the following page Derrida writes "Hochen Foda."

"Ein *Geschlecht*," "the only *betont* (emphasized) word in all of Trakl's oeuvre," this *Grundton* was, Heidegger said, the fundamental tone of the *Gedicht* and not of the *Dichtungen*. We can say, then, that the fundamental note is not spoken, it is kept quiet, which can mean two things: it is silent, in the sense that silence already belongs to speech or, another interpretation, unpronounced, unarticulated as articulate speech, it is sung, in a sense of the song that does not come down to, or is not reduced to the articulation of language, to that which in language is articulated. Now, Heidegger indeed spoke of the "danger of disturbing the saying of the poem, instead of letting it sing (*singen*) from its own proper repose."[2] If, in any case, the *Grundton* is on at least two occasions—at the beginning of the text and around the word "*Ein*" of "Ein *Geschlecht*"—assigned to the *Gedicht* and not to the *Dichtungen*, it is unspoken (I won't say unspeakable, so as not to introduce a prohibitive nuance that would lead us toward other scenes). But given that its unspokenness is not *something other* (elsewhere) than that which is spoken in the poems (*Dichtungen*), the question (and I raised it last week in response to Hachem Foda) concerning the relation between this singular unpronounced character and a determined idiom arises. It must be the case that, if the place of the unspoken *Gedicht* is not anything other than that to which it gives rise, it must be essentially affiliated [*apparenté*], in its very silence, to the German idiom, or even to Old High German. Its silence is German, it speaks German. But since in this silence, such as it is heard by Heidegger, it speaks German not only from a German place but from a place that, in turn, situates the place of the West, the Christian West as well as the West of Platonic and post-Platonic metaphysics—and thus of what Heidegger calls metaphysical theology—it must be the case that the German place here holds an absolute privilege both with respect to the Platonico-Christian West it allows us to think to the extent that it, too, belongs to it, and with respect

2. Heidegger, "Die Sprache im Gedicht," 35.

to this same West to the extent that it does not yet belong to it or already no longer belongs to it, which also allows it to think this West and say it. The absolute privilege of this place and this language—which I hesitate for reasons that are now obvious to call national (national place, national language)—is nevertheless that on the basis of which a nation as such can determine itself, present itself, name itself in the strict sense, even if, as Heidegger said in 1945, one must distinguish the national from nationalism.[3] Moreover, this absolute privilege of a place and a language is here implicitly afforded not only to *Dichten*, to the *Gedicht*, but to *Denken*, to thought, to the thinking that is in conversation with the poet and situates the place of his *Gedicht*.

On the question of *Gedicht*—the word *Gedicht* and its translation into French as "*Dict*" (D-I-C-T), a word that sometimes allows the translators to use the word "*dictée*" ["dictation"] for "*dichtendes Sagen*"[4]—I was vaguely aware, last Wednesday, that I was not being careful when I said that to my knowledge Heidegger never made this connection between Latin and German. I knew that I had read somewhere something pointing to this potential connection, but in the confusion of my memory I attributed it to the French translators attempting to justify their translation rather than to Heidegger. I was mistaken. All the more so given that it's in a Heidegger text I read recently that this connection, whatever it's worth, was proposed. No doubt it is attempted elsewhere. But I will just cite this passage because it concerns what we were saying a little while ago[5] about the hand, writing, and the typewriter. It is found in the seminar titled *Parmenides* (1942–43). Heidegger had just been speaking of the hand—I quoted this page before—then of handwriting (*Handschrift*) as the essence and essential origin of writing, and at the opening of a veritable

3. Martin Heidegger, *Reden und anderen Zeugnisse eines Lebensweges* (*GA* 16), ed. Hermann Heidegger (Frankfurt am Main: Vittorio Klostermann, 2000), 489; quoted in Derrida, *Psyche*, 2:32. See the preface, p. xxix.

4. Heidegger, 33.

5. See Derrida, *Psyche* 2:46–50.

indictment of the typewriter, which tears writing from the hand, from the essential realm of the hand, and thus of the word, the typewriter that "degrades (*degradiert*) the word [by reducing it] to a means of communication (*Verkehrsmittel*)," at the opening of this indictment to which we could return during discussion a little later, Heidegger writes: "It is not an accident that modern man writes 'with' [*mit*, in quotation marks: means, instrument, the pen would not be an instrument] the typewriter and 'dictates' [*diktiert*, in quotes] (*dasselbe Wort wie 'Dichten'*) 'in' (into) *die Maschine*."[6] And the following sentence speaks of a " 'history' of the kinds of writing (*'Geschichte' der Art des Schreibens*)" as a growing, progressive destruction of the word (*zunehmende Zerstörung des Wortes*)."[7] By putting *Dichten* next to *diktieren*, Heidegger does not only want to mark in general an etymological affinity between *Dichten* and this sort of order or injunction that one must listen to, to which a poet must give in, as to the source of his inspiration. In this precise context, *Dichten* and *diktieren* are brought together but also dissociated and demarcated. Dictation is a degeneration, a Latin corruption of *Dichten*; it is also the mechanical, machinic perversion of a *Dichten* that orders the saying without dictating it in the way one dictates to a secretary, a typewriter, or a tape recorder (this was written in 1942–43, and technical possibilities since then have only exacerbated what Heidegger obviously feels to be a danger for *Dichten*: Latin dictation (world of the juridical and the formal, of technics)).[8] Such that bringing these two together, at least in this context, justifies the translation of *Dichten* as "*dictée*" but also rejects it even more severely. But obviously, if we radicalize this logic—as we must do—it is the principle

6. Heidegger, *Parmenides*, trans. Andre Schuwer and Richard Rojcewicz (Bloomington: Indiana University Press, 1998), 81.
7. Heidegger, 119.
8. We close this parenthesis.

of a translation of Heidegger into a Romance language that is called into question. That is indeed what is at issue, and what, at bottom, we are constantly speaking of. So that's what I wanted to clarify with regard to the second of the three questions we encountered last time.

The third question led us toward what I had announced regarding the one, the unique, the gathering unicity of the *Ort* (indivisible tip of the spear), a question that I formulated more specifically last time as that of a difference between polysemy and dissemination. Before pursuing this question, a clarification on this word "indivisible" that I have used several times here and elsewhere, and which is not, as I said, Heidegger's word when he speaks of unity, the one, and the unique (*einzig*), or of gathering (*Versammlung*), which plays such a decisive role in this text and elsewhere. Heidegger would no doubt have protested against the word "indivisible." He would have protested for two reasons. He would have said, I imagine, that unity, simplicity, unicity (*Einzigkeit, Einfalt*), gathering (*Versammlung*), so many traits that for him characterize place (*Ort*) and the *Gedicht*, are not for all that indivisible, if the word "indivisible" seems to refer to the geometrical, objective punctuality of an area or the equally objective instantaneity of a time. He would object, perhaps, that even the tip of the spear (*die Spitze des Speers*) that serves for him as a reference, and even as a guarantee, for his determination of the word *Ort* does not have this geometrico-arithmetico-objective sense. Even if one could distinguish in this way between two senses of the tip [*pointe*] or of the point of the tip, two tips or two points in the sense of the point (good or bad polysemy?), nothing allows us to assign such limits to the word "indivisible" itself. It belongs to language, for example the French language, and can be used outside of its strictly mathematical context. There is no justification for, or absolute necessity of, condemning its signification to the domain of mathematization, and when I myself have happened to insist on the divisibility of the letter (in particular in a deconstructive reading[9] of Lacan's *Seminar on The Purloined Letter*), I was not limiting this word "divisibility" (no more than the word "dissemination") to its field of mathematizable objectivity. This is a first response to the objection I'm attributing to Heidegger. His second point of protest would perhaps have consisted in saying: the place or the *Gedicht* is not in*divisible*, it is possible for it to be divided, dissociated, even disseminated or decomposed—this is even the evil or curse I am talking about—but it remains indivisible in the sense that it mustn't or shouldn't be divided, it should be not divided. If division affects it, then this place is no longer intact, it is no longer the or a place, there are no longer grounds for speaking of place [*il n'y a plus lieu de parler de lieu*]. If there are grounds for speaking of place, if one desires place, if one is in motion toward place, then gathering, the movement of gathering, must prevail over dislocating forces. This is perhaps, at bottom, what Lacan would say of the letter as the place of the signifier that does "not [. . .] allow of partition."[10] We're touching here on what, metaphorically or ironically, I will call the great logic of the relations between deconstruction and the deconstructable. In recalling the divisibility of place, it is not a matter of insisting on the necessity or possibility of division happening to this place, affecting it in the manner of an evil and corrupting it. It is a matter of something else entirely, which I will schematize in the extreme in two arguments.

A. The fact, the factum or fatality of division *being able* to happen, the fact of this possibility (basically recognized by Heidegger), implies that the structure of that to which this can happen be such that this can happen to it. This happens, then, to its structure enough for one to be able

9. See above, p. 18, note 31.

10. Jacques Lacan, *Écrits: The First Complete Edition in English*, trans. Bruce Fink (New York: Norton, 2002), 16.

to say that this structure is essentially not indivisible but divisible. Moreover, in order for it to be able to gather itself or tend toward its gathering, it must be divisible, and this divisibility must not be merely an accident. Fundamentally, an accident does not happen if the essence cannot be affected by such an accident. If the essence is accidentable, it is *a priori* accidented. Whence the second argument.

B. This accident—here, divisibility—is not an evil, a simple evil. There would be no place, desire, or movement toward or from the place of gathering if this divisibility was excluded or extrinsic. It is, then, the essential condition of possibility and impossibility for desire or for place, here, for the *Gedicht*. Because, conversely, if the place or the letter were indivisible, unaffectable by dissociation, différance, etc., there would be no movement and thus no place and no letter, no *Gedicht* and no *Dichtung*. There would be even more negativity and evil than what gets attributed to divisibility, deconstruction, *différance*, or dissemination. It is the forces of death that would prevail even more certainly. If there were only gathering, sameness, oneness, place without path, that would be death without phrases [*la mort sans phrase*]. And this is not what Heidegger wants to say, since he also insists on movement, the path of the stranger, the path toward others, and so on. It must be, then, that relations be otherwise between place and non-place, gathering and divisibility (*différance*), that a sort of negotiation and compromise be continuously underway that requires us to rework the implicit logic that seems to be guiding Heidegger. To say that there is divisibility does not come down to saying that there is only divisibility or division either (that, too, would be death). Death lies in wait on both sides, on the side of the phantasm of the integrity of the proper place and the innocence of a sexual difference without war, and, on the opposite side, that of a radical impropriety or expropriation, or even a war of *Geschlecht* as sexual discord. I don't use the word "phantasm" lightly, as if we already knew what the phantasm is all about thanks to psychoanalysis. No, on the contrary, the point is to elaborate the concept of phantasm on the basis of this "great logic," which I say here ironically because what I want to say is that the most continuous great logic of philosophy, the one that presupposes an exteriority between essence and accident, pure and impure, proper and improper, good and evil, this great logic remains at work in Heidegger (see what he says about logos as gathering) in spite of everything, in spite of powerful deconstructive movements in Heidegger against the great logic of Hegel.[11]

All right, this was just a reminder and a slightly long transition from what was said last week and two weeks ago.

Let's try now to go, if you will, a bit further or a bit closer, as you like.

In the name of the plurivocity of language or speech (*Mehrdeutigkeit der Sprache*), of this good plurivocity that must be gatherable into the simplicity of the *Einklang* and the *Grundton*, the harmonic unity and the fundamental tone, Heidegger recognizes that there are in Trakl's vocabulary, in the words of his corpus, in his *Dichtungen* if not in his *Gedicht*:

[. . .] expressions that belong to the biblical and ecclesiastical world of representation [and not, as the French translation says, "to Biblical and religious or ecclesiastical representations of the world" [for *Vorstellungswelt*] (*Worte, die zur biblischen and kirchlichen Vorstellungswelt gehören*)]. The transition from the old *Geschlecht* to the unborn crosses

11. The end of this sentence, which contains an interlinear addition, reads in the typescript: "this grand logic that remains in spite of everything at work, in spite of powerful deconstructive movements in Heidegger against the grand logic of Hegel (see what he says about Logos as gathering) in Heidegger."

[leads through, *führt durch*] this domain and its language [in other words, the Christian domain and its language, its code].[12]

Heidegger recognizes this but only within the context of polysemy, a polysemy that has led critics to speak of Trakl's Christianity or his properly Christian inspiration. But Heidegger will attempt to reduce this polysemy by demonstrating that Trakl is not Christian, or, more rigorously, that the place from which he speaks or to which his poems tend to return as to their source, his *Gedicht*, is not the Christian place.

How does Heidegger claim to show this? At first he seems very cautious. He says that these are essential questions.

> Whether, to what extent, and in what sense Trakl's poetry speaks in a Christian way (*christlich spricht*), in what way the poet was "*Christ*," what "Christian," "Christianity," "Christendom," "Christianness" (*Christlichkeit*) mean here and in general, all this contains [or entails, *schließt ein*] essential questions. But [Heidegger adds, very rightly and still very cautiously] the situation of these questions [I don't know why this time the French translators translate *Erörterung* in such a banal way as "discussion"] will be suspended in the void as long as the place (*Ort*) of the *Gedicht* has not been considered. Moreover, this situation requires a deliberation (*Nachdenken*) for which either the concepts of metaphysical theology or those of a church-based [ecclesiastical] theology are insufficient.

Despite his discretion and his caution, such an assertion remains rather violent and, I will say once more, rather dogmatic. For, to say that the concepts of theology (metaphysical or dogmatic theology: that is to say, in short, all of metaphysics, period [*LA métaphysique*], which is an onto-theology, and

12. Heidegger, "Die Sprache im Gedicht," 72.

all of theology, period [*LA théologie*], which constituted itself even as Christian theology by integrating or translating pre-Christian Greek metaphysics; and we must say metaphysics, period, since elsewhere in the same text, following the same type of argument, Heidegger says the same thing about the metaphysics that descended from Plato, which here includes Aristotelian metaphysics, which played the role you are familiar with in an entire dimension of Christian theology), to say, then, "neither the concepts of metaphysical theology nor those of eccelesiastical theology are sufficient," one must presuppose that these concepts have a univocal sense or a masterable, gatherable plurivocity, that these concepts of theology, metaphysics, and dogmatics also have a place that is one and from which one can say "this is not Trakl's place, Trakl's *Gedicht*," or "this is not a place commensurate with the place of Trakl's *Gedicht*." But what would happen if we were not in agreement on this point, if we rejected this presupposition, if we said: there is not only one place for this thing called Metaphysics or Theology, or, what's more, if we want to access the Place of texts, the place from which so-called metaphysical or Christian texts proceed, we must stop believing in a certain univocity and read them how we read Trakl, by giving them the same credit. Perhaps they say the same thing as Trakl, perhaps they say something entirely different from what Heidegger believes they say when he declares their overall inadequacy when it comes to the situation of Trakl's *Gedicht*. We can imagine that in the name of an authentically Christian place, a thought claims as Christian, more Christian than others, Trakl's texts that Heidegger wants to shield from Christianity, up to and including everything that is said of *Geschlecht*. All the more easily given that, as we already noted, the entire content of Heidegger's interpretation of the two blows (the good and the bad), of the two sexual differences (before and after the curse), everything he says about evil and the bad resembles Christian content to the point of being mistaken for it. Except that Heidegger distinguishes, as it were, the Christian or even Platonic fact from that which must have made it possible, by being more originary. But this more originary is nothing other, in its content, than that which it makes possible and which proceeds from it. In order to think Platonism and Christianity, in order to think their possibility, says Heidegger in short, it is necessary to go back to a situation that is not yet Platonico-Christian, out of which the emergence of Platonico-Christianity was possible, and a thought of the curse, evil, corruption, and so on. But in this more originary situation there is nothing other than that which became Platonico-Christian. It is the status of this repetition that seems to me highly problematic in Heidegger.[13]

I understand "repetition" in the strongest, most active, most violent sense of the term, which entails a demand, a questioning, a petition in reiteration. Such a repetition can be claimed by Christian thinkers who may no doubt seem unorthodox, but who thereby claim to shake Christianity out of a dogmatic slumber and thus to be more authentically Christian. I am thinking here not only of Kierkegaard[14] but also of modern Christian "theologians" or exegetes,[15] Protestant or Catholic, or also, since Heidegger speaks of the biblical in general, of modern Jewish theologians, the very ones who are sometimes accused of being dissidents or atheists, reeking of heresy. They don't need Christian or biblical words or code, the usual marks of recognition, the signs by which one recognizes a Christian discourse, by which a certain Christianity recognizes itself in its discourse. Because the evidence or the signs that Heidegger seems to rely on in order to say that Trakl was not a Christian poet are quite simply the absence of certain words or themes in Trakl's *Dichtungen*. What would he say to someone who would protest in the name of the unspoken *Gedicht*, precisely, and who would answer back: no doubt

---

13. Handwritten addition: "Do not simplify . . . *Zwiefach*."
14. In the typescript: "KKG."
15. Marginal addition: "inspired by H<eidegger>."

the word "God" or the name "Christ" are not spoken by the *Dichtungen,* no doubt the theme of Christian redemption or hope is not literally named by Trakl, but does that prove that his place or his *Gedicht* isn't Christian? This silence signifies, perhaps, a more rigorous repetition of Christianity, a more rigorous and demanding return to the source or originary place.

Look, indeed, at what Heidegger says:

> A judgment concerning the Christianness of Trakl's poem would have to consider above all his final two poems, "Lament" ("Klage") and "Grodck" [why only the final two, a classical critic would say, but let's move on]. It would have to ask [Heidegger continues]: why does the poet here, in the utmost distress of his final saying, not call on God or Christ, if he is such a resolute Christian [so decidedly Christian, *wenn er ein so entschiedener Christ ist*]?[16]

The question is a bit much, as is a bit much the objection to those who would want, rightly or wrongly, to consider Trakl a Christian poet (I am not defending that thesis but rather analyzing Heidegger's strategy and what is problematic about it—which deserves to be questioned). The question and the objection are a bit much, not to mention a bit crude. For three reasons.

1. It presupposes or pretends to presuppose that a Christian must name God and Christ, and that if these words are absent—or are not heard, and one could confront Heidegger with everything he himself says, with such refinement and insistence, on silence as speech, the speech in silence or the silence in speech: a name is perhaps even more audible, in certain situations and certain ways of speaking, if it is not spoken. And Heidegger does not refrain elsewhere from making us understand [*entendre*] the unspoken as

16. Heidegger, "Die Sprache im Gedicht," 72.

the essential part of what is thought, or even from making us understand the unthought as the essential part of that which gives itself to be thought and which provokes thinking. I imagine, too, someone saying that the silence that keeps the names of God and Christ quiet lets Christianity be thought better than all the sermons and treatises on Christian theology. And that thus letting the possibility of Christianity be thought is perhaps more authentically Christian than a priest, a pastor, or a theologian. Moreover, why at the moment of death (here it's a question of the death of Trakl himself, the poet, since these are his last poems) should the "names" of God and Christ be inevitable, inevitably invoked, called out by an authentic Christian<?> And what is an authentic Christian? This brings me to the second reason.

2. I underscored *entschiedener Christ*. Heidegger asks why such a resolute, decided, determined Christian does not pronounce the names of Christ or God with his last breath. He seems to suppose with this that a Christian or a man of faith in general can and must be "resolute" or "decided," can and must be what he is unequivocally, and nothing else. No more polysemy, no more indecision all of a sudden: either you're Christian or you're not, and if you are, you don't forget to name God and Christ. Nevertheless— and Heidegger knows this, should have taken it into account, knows it better than anyone given his training, his itinerary, his theological culture, etc.—a Christian and a man of faith in general is not necessarily a man of certainty, a man with unshakable and unshakably constant resolution. A faith without anxiety, without indecision, without an experience of the withdrawal of God and even of the name of God or Christ would not be a faith, precisely, an authentically Christian one, or even a faith *tout court*.[17]

---

17. Marginal addition: "Either you're Christian or you're not, for heaven's sake, H<eidegger> seems to say."

This is so obvious and so well-known that you'll forgive me for not providing examples. What I really want to mark here, having to do with Heidegger's strategy and his manner (his hand), is that in order to assign or recognize the unequivocal place of Trakl's *Gedicht*, he has to presuppose that this place has not only a unicity and an indivisible gathering, but he also has to attribute these characteristics (gathering and indivisibility) to the places that are not, which Heidegger claims are not those of Trakl's *Gedicht*, for example the Christian place or the place of metaphysical theology. Now, what I said under the ironic heading of the "great logic" a minute ago, namely, the impure relation of contamination between divisibility and indivisibility, différance and dissemination, holds just as much for metaphysics and Christianity as for that from which one wishes to distinguish them.

3. Third reason: Heidegger's request and objection are quite excessive because this time, contrary to what he does elsewhere in the same text, he refers to the poet himself, the living poet, the life of the poet on the brink of his death, the experience of Georg Trakl, and he permits himself to draw a conclusion from poem to poem: if Trakl were, as you say, Christian, a Christian poet, his final poem should bear the trace of this and name God or Christ. As if 1. a Christian poet (in his soul and in his life) were not able not to name God in his final poems, as if the poems had to express, manifest, reflect immediately, directly, the poet's state of mind, and as if, 2. (here I'm repeating what I was saying a moment ago in another way) as if the presence or absence of the names of God and Christ had to testify not only to the Christian or non-Christian character of the poem, of what is said in the saying (*Sagen*), or even of the unspoken *Gedicht*, but even of the Christian or non-Christian character of the poet. Here, I believe the obstinacy in shielding Trakl, and himself, Heidegger, in his reading of Trakl and elsewhere—because we have many other signs, from

the beginning, in Heidegger's thought of this demarcation with respect to Christianity and Christian theology—the obstinacy in shielding Trakl and shielding himself from a "place" of Christian thought pushes Heidegger to simplify excessively, sometimes counter to what he himself cautions, and to fall back into the most familiar ruts (but is there a path of thought without ruts?).

The rest of the demonstration—the rest of the paragraph in which Heidegger claims to dismiss, as it were, those who want to make Trakl a Christian poet and thus his thinking of *Geschlecht* a Christian thinking or poetry—is also, in my opinion, "insufficient," to use Heidegger's word when he qualifies the concepts of dogmatic or metaphysical theology (*nicht zureichen*). What, indeed, does Heidegger say? He says it again in the form of a false question: why doesn't Trakl say that if he is Christian? Why, instead of that, does he say this other thing which, it is implied, is not Christian. Why, for example, instead of naming God and Christ does he "name the wavering shadow of the sister (*den schwankenden Schatten der Schwester*), and the latter as 'the greeter' [as the French translation says for *als die grüßende*, 'she who greets,'[18] says the poem]?"[19] Strange. First of all, it is not clear why this would come instead of the name of Christ (*statt dessen*), and even if it does come in its stead, is it such an un-Christian metonymy that would replace the name of Christ, son of God, and the name of God, father of Christ, with the name of the sister? If you gave me a little time, I would undertake what would not be just an exercise, what is on the contrary a very serious thing that could be experienced with fear and trembling, but which might today become a mere exercise, which would consist in demonstrating that the figure of the sister and that of Christ can very easily be substituted for one another. And precisely

18. Trakl, "Grodek," 72.
19. Heidegger, 72.

in Trakl's corpus, if I may say so. How is one to determine the sex of Christ, and how is one to characterize, within sexual difference, the properly Christian, decidedly Christian experience that a man (supposing that Trakl is a man, decidedly a man, "one-sidedly a man," as one of Joyce's commentators dared to say of him) or a woman has of the relation to Christ? The son of God, Christ is brother to all men and women, at the same time as he is the image or intercessor of the father. But a brother whose virility is never simply manifest or unilateral, a brother who presents himself in an aura of universal homosexuality, or in a peaceful, pacified (gentle, Trakl would say) sexual difference, outside the moment of temptation where evil is near, a brother, then, who is perhaps no different than a sister. And the sexual determination of a son born of a virgin, herself born of an immaculate conception, cannot be sure enough that one can blithely say: where the poet names the sister instead of Christ he does not name Christ, he is not Christian, or what's more, his poem is not Christian. This is all the more impossible or hasty given that Heidegger himself does not fail to call attention to this strange couple of brother and sister in Trakl's poems. I say "couple" because it testifies to a sexual difference that, though it is not yet or is already no longer that of war or discord, sexual difference as antagonism (*Zwietracht*), is nevertheless not without desire, in the sense that Hegel said (about Antigone) that the relation between brother and sister was *begierdelos*: perhaps without manifest desire in the space where desire makes war, after the second blow, but not without gentle desire, a relation to the other as double homosexuality, a reflection without appropriation of the desire of the other in which the brother becomes the sister and the sister the brother, etc. And whoever can blithely affirm that this is not the essence of the relation to Christ, the essence or at least the destination, the destiny that is sought after, toward which every Christian experience of the holy family, or even the family *tout court*, is on the way? (See *Glas*? I allow myself to cite this title only because it is at the moment of Trakl's death that Heidegger reminds those who make Trakl into a Christian that he should have spoken of Christ and God and not the sister, a sister who is always the sister with "the voice of the moon [*mondene Stimme*, the 'selenic voice,' as the French translation says] that always resonates in the spiritual night," as the final lines (*eschaton*, as well) of *Geistliche Dämmerung* (eschatological figure of the sister) say. Is this selenic figure of the sister (the *eschaton*, the nocturnal light that greets one, etc.) so foreign to the figure of Christ? And is Christ, like the sister, a figure whose meaning is so decidable? I could continue on this path; it's neither indispensable nor very economical.)[20] The end of the paragraph is even more surprising and emphatic in this same sense. More surprising because it banks on a distinction or an opposition that is more fragile than ever, that of a confidence in Christian redemption, on the one hand, and the naming of the "*ungeborenen Enkel* [unborn *neveux* or descendants]" on the other. Heidegger writes: "Why does the song not end on the confident prospect of Christian redemption [literally: with the confident view or perspective, *mit dem zuversichtlichen Ausblick auf die christliche Erlösung*, of Christian redemption] [. . .]?"[21] But, precisely, here too one may very well interpret otherwise, and in a less conventional way, Christian redemption and eschatology and hear in everything Heidegger says to us about the "unborn descendants" and the more originary *Geschlecht* still to come the most authentically Christian discourse there is. One could respond in the same way to the arguments that close this paragraph: "Why does the sister [Heidegger asks again] also appear in the other final poem, 'Lament'?"[22] But why not, especially if she is not decidably opposable to Christ or if, distinct from the figure of Christ, it is not necessarily a-Christian or anti-Christian to name her insistently. Finally,

20. We close the parenthesis here.
21. Heidegger, "Die Sprache im Gedicht," 72.
22. Heidegger, 72.

especially if a poem does something other than to translate in a decidable way the univocal thought or experience of a poet. A poet can write or describe the lament without lamenting; he can, moreover, quote one poem in another, or another poet, be Christian without writing Christian poems or write Christian poems without being Christian. Above all, he or the poem can be Christian without being so, or without knowing it, or without wanting it. Once again, being or not being Christian is perhaps not such a univocal and decidable thing, as Heidegger suddenly seems to require in his questions and objections about a poet said to be—but the expression is Heidegger's own—"*ein so entschiedener Christ. . . .*"[23] How would Heidegger have responded to a Christian saying to him: to be Christian is not a position, an identity, nor a state, nor even a being [*être*] and its gatherable essence. To be Christian is something else, and it greatly resembles, to the point of being mistaken for it, what you are and what you say Trakl is in his place. It is possible for a Christian to speak of eternity (here I'm alluding to the argument that Heidegger makes next) "as a glacial swell (*die Ewigkeit, die eisige Woge*)."[24] This Christian without being one would then say to Heidegger: and when you ask if this is a Christian thought, if "this is thought in a Christian manner (*Ist das christlich gedacht?*)," well, sure, why not?[25] In any event, it's not clear under what aegis one can decide whether it is or not without some other recourse.

Finally, when Heidegger concludes in a very decided way: "It is not even Christian despair (*Es ist nicht einmal christliche Verzweiflung*)," he presupposes that the despair of a "Christian" (but, again, what is a Christian?) must remain Christian, Christian enough in its form to retain its identity as Christian despair. But when a Christian despairs, I imagine that he de-

23. Marginal addition: "Faith = to decide in the indecidable [two or three indecipherable words, perhaps 'or is nothing']."

24. Heidegger, "Die Sprache im Gedicht," 72.

25. Heidegger, 72.

spairs first and foremost (and I am sure that we could find numerous texts to back this up) that he can no longer recognize the form of Christian despair in his despair. The Christian despairs of Christianity, or else he doesn't really despair. He despairs as a Christian precisely when he despairs of no longer even being able to give a Christian form to his despair, so he despairs as a Christian when he despairs of Christianity. A Shiite has never despaired of Christianity. But neither has a Christian, as long as he despairs in forms that are Christian and identifiable as such. Can we be sure that in the moment of his greatest despair Christ—to name only him—experienced a *christliche Verzweiflung*? Yes and no. (The *Zwei* of *Verzweiflung*, see Hegel,[26] doubt, two . . .)

Naturally, keeping to a tight and internal examination of this paragraph, I will not take advantage of the all too easy opportunity to recall that, outside of these final poems, Trakl often names God and even Lucifer, in passages that Heidegger himself cited.

Next time we will return to this question of knowing what Heidegger is doing here, what repetition he engages in, what story he is telling, what he makes of speech and silence. And then we will come back to the question of the "one" of "Ein *Geschlecht*" in the short, final part of the text.

---

26. See Georg Wilhelm Friedrich Hegel, *Phänomenologie des Geistes*, ed. E. Moldenhauer and K. Michel (Frankfurt am Main: Suhrkamp, 1970), 72.

Eleventh Session

Some of you may be asking yourselves whether this rather meticulous and microscopic attention we've been paying to the letter of a Heidegger text on a poet over the past several weeks doesn't take us far from our subject and the great questions of philosophical nationality or nationalism. Well, if there are those among you who are worried about this, they are mistaken. Not only have we never left the places that are, in my opinion, the most decisive for all these great and burning questions, but even if we have done so, today we are back, back in the home country. Today we will be talking about the "country" (*Land*), still in Heidegger's text on Trakl. Because the discipline I believed I had to impose on myself here, so as to avoid any dispersion and concentrate all our attention on the tightest links in the text, is to confine myself to it for a certain amount of time and not to invoke, as would be necessary to do in a different situation, either other Heidegger texts (I have hardly cited a single one), or other Trakl texts, or, *a fortiori*, other texts on Heidegger or Trakl. For example, for everything I am going to say today about the country, it would be necessary, were I not following this rule, provisionally, to take into account the constant and direct, sometimes overwhelming presence of Hölderlin behind all these texts, Trakl's as well as Heidegger's. Perhaps one day I will talk about Hölderlin directly in this seminar, but if I planned to talk about him seriously today, it would be an endless detour that would take us away for too long from this text that we are interested in right now. Those who are familiar with Hölderlin will recognize all the nods made by Trakl, Heidegger, and myself reading them, toward the motif of the "country" or what is called the homeward turn (*Kehre*) in Hölderlin, the question of the Occident (Hesperia) and Greece in his work and in the texts Heidegger dedicates to him, and so on. Here I'm thinking not only of the *Erläuterungen zu Hölderlins Dichtung*[1] (1951—distinguish from *Eine Erörterung von Georg Trakls Gedicht*) and of all the allusions to Hölderlin here and there, but very specifically of what is said in the *Letter on Humanism*, which I will remind you dates from 1946. Everything I will be emphasizing and interrogating today concerning this "country" and the Occident (*Abendland*) is announced, precisely, apropos of Hölderlin in the *Letter*. Here is a mere indication, a kind of parenthesis or epigraph, then we will get back to the text on Trakl. In the *Letter*, Heidegger opposes Hölderlin to Winckelmann, Goethe, and Schiller, men of eighteenth-century humanism, whereas "Hölderlin does not belong to 'humanism' [to that humanism], precisely because he thinks the destiny of the essence of the human being in a more originary way than this 'humanism' is able to."[2] It is this journey toward the more originary that we are going to track starting now. In a particular passage from the *Letter*, Heidegger, who has already set against the human being of metaphysical humanism—who is still an animal (sometimes thought biologically, even if one adds those properties that language, reason, etc. would be)—a certain pro-

1. Martin Heidegger, *Erläuterungen zu Hölderlins Dichtung* (*GA* 4), ed. Friedrich-Wilhelm von Hermann (1951; Frankfurt am Main: Vittorio Klostermann, 1981). Published in English as Martin Heidegger, *Elucidations of Hölderlin's Poetry*, trans. Keith Hoeller (Amherst, NY: Humanity Books, 2000).

2. Heidegger, "Brief über den 'Humanismus,'" in *Wegmarken*, 320; Heidegger, "Letter on 'Humanism,'" in *Pathmarks*, 244 (translation modified slightly here and below).

jection of the human, a projection (*Entwurf*) on the basis of which an essence of the human is decided that is not reducible to that of classical humanism, of the *zōon logon echon* or the *animal rationale*.[3] This projection (*Entwurf*), this thrown (*geworfener*) projection is not thrown by the human. "What throws [the throwing, *das Werfende*] in such projection is not the human being but being itself, which sends [*schickt*, which destines] the human being into the ek-sistence of *Da-sein* that is his essence."[4] It is a question of knowing what or who sends the most originarily. Heidegger says, it is being that sends the human and destines him to the There, to being there: it is being that sends or destines (*schickt*) the human being to the there, to being there. "This destiny [or this gathering of the sending] propriates (*ereignet*) as the clearing of being (*Lichtung des Seins*)—which it is. The clearing grants nearness to being."[5] It is in this nearness (and it is a question, then, of thinking nearness, and without thinking nearness one cannot think country, nation, language, etc.) that the human dwells. To dwell is to be in this proximity of the *Lichtung* and the *Da*. It is with this reminder that Heidegger ties, as it were, his discourse to Hölderlin's poem, to his poetry. "This nearness 'of' being [double genitive and quotes: explain]," which is in itself the 'there' (*Da*) of *Dasein*, Heidegger calls it *Heimat*, homeland, in his lecture on "Heimkunft" ("Homecoming"), the Hölderlin elegy.[6] Heidegger then explains that he is using Hölderlin's word (*Heimat*) to designate the there of being there and a proximity that he already described using other names in *Sein und Zeit*.

> The word *Heimat* (homeland) [Heidegger says, in a desire for precision and clarity that matters greatly for us here,

3. Sentence as such in the typescript.
4. Heidegger, "Letter on 'Humanism,'" 257.
5. Heidegger, 257.
6. Heidegger, 257.

from the point of view of this seminar, and which also matters greatly in 1946, the date of the *Letter*] is thought here in
an essential way [in an essential sense, *in einem wesentlichen
Sinne*], not patriotically or nationalistically [note that these
last two words are used in their Latinity, as is always the
case when it comes to being pejorative; they are implicitly
sent back to their Latin family, their Romance *Geschlecht,
nicht patriotisch, nicht nationalistich*] but in terms of the
history of being (*seinsgeschichtlich*). [And Heidegger adds:]
The essence of the homeland (*das Wesen der Heimat*) is also
mentioned with the intention of thinking the homelessness
of contemporary human beings (*die Heimatlosigkeit des
neuzeitlichen Menschen*) from out of the essence of the history of being. Nietzsche was the last to experience this *Heimatlosigkeit*. From within metaphysics he was unable to find
any other way out than a reversal of metaphysics. But that
is the height of futility [he closed off all avenues, all paths,
because he remained within metaphysics; he tried to find a
path by inverting metaphysics, but that was the very com-
pletion of the closing, of the no-way-out, the no-path out,
das aber ist Vollendung der Ausweglosigkeit, comment . . .].
Hölderlin [he, on the other hand, did not close off the path,
did not close himself off in metaphysics], on the other hand,
when he poetizes "*Heimkunft*" [the homecoming], is concerned that his "*Landesleute*" [his "countrymen"] find their
essence in it [*ihr Wesen finden*, and this essence is not that
of nationality or the people]. He does not at all seek that essence [says Heidegger] in an egoism of his people (*in einem
Egoismus seines Volkes*). He sees it rather in the context of a
belongingness to the destiny of the West (*Zugehörigkeit in
das Geschick des Abendlandes*).[7]

This remark matters greatly to us for situating the text on
Trakl and what is there underscored or selected, as it were

7. Heidegger, 257.

(by Trakl and Heidegger alike, by Trakl in his two poems bearing *Abendland* in the title, and by Heidegger in several very important moments in his reading). But what is the Occident? Heidegger says of it what he said of *Heimat*: it must not be thought in a "regional" way (again a Latin word: *nicht regional*), and the regional here is the Occident in contrast to the Levant or the Orient, as the *Couchant*.[8] That is not the Occident, and it is not even Europe. It is necessary to think the Occident or Europe on the basis of the history of being or "world-historically out of nearness to the origin (*aus der Nähe zum Ursprung*)."[9] This nearness to the origin, with all the topological paradoxes to which it may give rise, will command the entire "logic" of the text on Trakl and the interpretation of the Occident in his poems. Having just named the Orient or the Levant in the *Letter*, and having noted that it is necessary to think it not as a region but from the history of the world and the history of being, Heidegger adds: "We have still scarcely begun to think the mysterious relations to the East (*geheimnisvollen Bezüge zum Osten*) that have come to word (*Wort*) in Hölderlin's poetry [question of the Orient and the Far-East in Hölderlin: explain . . .].[10]

Attentive to the fact that this discourse, especially in 1946, resonates from its proximity to the question of German nationalism, Heidegger inverts things, or believes he is inverting things and eliminating the suspicion of German nationalism, whereas, I believe, he does nothing but reproduce the ambiguity or equivocality of every nationalist discourse, in particular, in this context, the Fichtean discourse the basic schema of which we at least identified, which is obviously not a vulgarly

---

8. The French word *couchant* designates the place where the sun sets—the West—as well as the setting sun or sunset; it also carries a literary sense of old age or decline. Derrida uses the word here in contrast to *Levant*, the East, where the sun rises. (—Trans.)

9. Heidegger, 257.

10. Heidegger, 257.

nationalist schema but a call, beyond race, territory, State, and even language, to the German nation so that it may emerge from its impotence, isolation, and abstraction, it being understood that only what desires the infinite progress of freedom will be properly German, that is, only what responds to a non-empirical, non-empirico-national calling. Now, what does Heidegger say here, just after emphasizing that the Occident is not the *Couchant*, the region where the sun sets, nor even Europe, but must be thought on the basis of the history of the world and the history of being? He names Germany, he names German, Germanity, *das "Deutsche,"* in quotes (quotation), which is badly translated as "German reality": it is Germanness, Germanity, as well as the German language, all the more so given that at issue in the sentence is German such as it is spoken to the world (*der Welt gesagt*). Indeed: "'German' (*das 'Deutsche'*) is not spoken to the world so that the world might be healed through the German essence (*damit sie am deutschen Wesen genese*); rather, it is spoken to the Germans so that from a destinal belongingness to other peoples they might become world-historical along with them."[11] This is indeed the sense of Fichte's gesture, at least to a certain extent, that of the address to the German people. Fichte does not say to other peoples: German is going to come heal you or redeem you. He speaks to the Germans, it is a speech to a German nation that in some sense has not yet come or come back into its own and which finds itself called to think itself, to think the German within a universal teleological horizon (that of spiritual freedom). So, naturally, the history of the world and of being, for Heidegger, is not this spiritualist teleology and metaphysical freedom (also that of Husserl in the *Crisis of European Sciences* and of European humanity; fiftieth anniversary soon in Vienna) but the formal schema of the gesture is the same, to think the German from an origin

11. Heidegger, 257.

or horizon that exceeds it, to address the German in a non-regional, non-"national"—empirico-national—sense. Nevertheless, from this nearness of being that is the homeland of this historical dwelling, one must not efface the homeland, or the German; one must not give way to an empty universalism, a cosmopolitanism that would be the symmetrical and negative opposite of nationalism, a cosmopolitanism often associated with the Enlightenment. At bottom, cosmopolitanism and nationalism, internationalism and nationalism would be two symmetrical and fundamentally indifferent versions of the same humanist metaphysics.[12] We confirmed the necessity of this schema on several occasions during the first trimester without reference at that point to Heidegger. If I did not refer to Heidegger then, it is because I suspected, and still suspect, Heidegger of not escaping the formality of this schema when he calls us to think the homeland from the origin and horizon of the history of being and the world, and when he places the human qua *Dasein* in this place more originary than the human of metaphysical humanism qua *animal rationale*, or when he laments *Heimatlosigkeit* as the destiny of the world and as an effect of metaphysics, and when he writes the following, for example:

The world-historical thinking of Hölderlin that speaks out in the poem "Andenken" is essentially more original (*anfänglicher*) and thus more significant for the future (*und deshalb zukünftiger*) than the mere cosmopolitanism of Goethe (*als das bloße Weltbürgertum Goethes*). For the same reason Hölderlin's relation to Hellenism is something essentially other than humanism [earlier <in the *Letter*>, Goethe's humanist Hellenism; later, Marx's depth: alienation as *Heimatlosigkeit*, better than Husserl and Sartre].[13]

12. Heidegger, "Brief über den 'Humanismus,'" 338; "Letter on 'Humanism,'" xx.
13. "Brief über den 'Humanismus,'" 339; "Letter on 'Humanism,'" 258.

The logic that we will find at work in the text on Trakl we see already at work here, and it is an omnipresent "logic" in Heidegger's approach: what is more originary bears more future, the more originary is more to come—and although this has a circular form, it would need to be thought beyond, more originarily and more futurally (?)[14] than the Hegelian dialectical circle that belongs to that Occidental-European logic beyond or on this side of which one must carry oneself; circle of the circle?

Just as when he says "*Ortschaft des Ortes*" (in the Trakl text) Heidegger is not thinking the locality of the place abstractly, the essence of place, but the concrete—the word *Ortschaft*, in everyday language, also means landscape, region, village, locality in the sense that, in French, one says this or that *localité* in order to speak of a specific place in a concrete area—likewise here, when he says "German," and German beyond the homeland determined by patriotism or nationalism, he nevertheless means something very concrete. The proof is the sentence in the *Letter* that immediately follows the one about Goethe, cosmopolitanism, and Hölderlin's relation to Hellenism as something other than a humanism: "When confronted with death, therefore, those young Germans who knew about Hölderlin (*die von Hölderlin wußten*) lived and thought something other (*Anderes*) than what the general public [*Öffentlichkeit*: the public sphere] held to be the typical German attitude (*als deutsche Meinung ausgab*). [Comment.]"[15] I return now to the point where we left off at the end of the last session, and we come to the country, *das Land*.

The end of the second part[16] recapitulates the movement after having shielded, or claimed to shield, Trakl's *Gedicht* from Christianity and metaphysics, from metaphysical as well as dogmatic theology. Trakl's plurivocity, his plurivocal speech

---

14. As such in the typescript.
15. "Brief über den 'Humanismus,'" 339; "Letter on 'Humanism,'" 258.
16. Heidegger, "Die Sprache im Gedicht," 76.

(*mehrstimmigen Sprache*) has found its rigorous unison, its harmony (*Einklang*). Trakl's *Dichtung* speaks from this unison, which means at the same time that it keeps something quiet or keeps itself quiet, remains tacit (*schweigt*), just as the *Gedicht* remains tacit. In this speaking silence or this tacit speech Trakl's poetry corresponds, it responds, it attunes itself (*entspricht*) to the *Abgeschiedenheit*, to the Dis-cease, to the departure that is not death even though in everyday language, and in keeping with the equivocation, the word means decease, death. This Dis-cease, this departure is the place of the *Gedicht*.[17] We must pay close attention to this: the place here is de-parture, not death, but that which, resembling death, is only dis-cease, departure toward that more originary morning of a mark, of a *Geschlecht* to come. The place is not a spot, a location one settles into, a place of stability, it is a departure, already a difference. This is what is difficult to think, and it's why, after having said that the place of the *Gedicht* is departure, Heidegger adds that to pay proper attention to this place, "to *consider* this place corrrectly (*diesen Ort recht zu beachten*) already provokes thought [and not, as it is translated, 'demands much from thinking': Heidegger says *gibt schon zu denken*]."[18] It provokes thought [*donne à penser*] only because it is not thinkable, it is not easy to think, a place that dis-locates itself, as it were, immediately, originarily, a place not as a residence but as a de-parture, a place one does not inhabit by choosing to reside there but that one dwells in by departing—from departure in a certain way—by parting ways with it in order to reappropriate it: a place, in short, that is split [*partagé*], in the double sense of the word, that to which one belongs or which belongs in common in gathering, and that which separates or is split. *Le lieu se partage* ["Place is split"], we would say in French to translate without translating *Abgeschiedenheit* as place. As it is difficult to think that

17. Heidegger, 76.
18. Heidegger, 72.

which provokes thought here—and only the unthinkable can provoke thought—Heidegger concludes this second part with a "hardly": "We can hardly dare, in conclusion, to question after the locality of this place (*nach der Ortschaft dieses Ortes*)":[19] *Ortschaft* at once concrete and abstract, hence the word "country" (*Land*), which will not take long to appear starting at the beginning of the third part. This "locality" is the country, a country. It is the country of a promise (*Versprechen*). The word "promise" seems to me to be essential from this point forward, and we will see it show up at the same time as the word "country."

Thus we approach the third part. This one seems to close a circle and return to the beginning of the text, namely, toward the penultimate stanza of the poem "Autumn Soul" ("Herbstseele") quoted at the very beginning:

> Soon fish and game slide away.
> Blue soul, darksome journey.
> Soon severed us from loved ones, others (*schied uns bald*
> *von Lieben, Andern*).[20]

This stanza names the wanderers who follow the path of the stranger [his track, *Pfad*, his trail] through the spiritual night in order to [quote] *in "beseelter Bläue wohnen"* [in order to inhabit this blue that is animate, endowed with a soul, to *"trouver demeure"* ["find dwelling"], says the French translation, *"en son azur doué d'âme"* ["in its blue endowed with a soul"]].[21]

Now, what promises or grants a habitat, a dwelling, *Wohnen*, what promises (*verspricht*) it and grants it, keeps it (*gewährt*)

19. Heidegger, 73.
20. Trakl, "Herbstseele," quoted in Heidegger, 73; Trakl, "Autumn Soul," in *Poems and Prose*, 66/67.
21. Heidegger, 73.

it, is what "our language (*unsere Sprache*) calls *das 'Land.'*"²²
Once again, the word "*Land*" is a word from our language; to
translate it with country, fatherland, territory, etc. would be
to miss everything that is given and promised in the word of
our language, *Land*. In other words, the country (*das Land*)
can really only be said in the language of our "*Land*," and not
of our country. It is again the same logic we saw at work with
so many words, in particular and *par excellence* the word
Sinn, sinnan (comment: there was also *fram, fremd, Ort, Geist,
Wahnsinn*, and several others).

Having thus appropriated, reappropriated the word "*Land*,"
Heidegger adds a clarification that will decide everything.
"The passage [*Überschritt*: literally the step beyond [*le pas au-
delà*]] into the land of the stranger happens through the spiritual twilight of the evening, in the evening (*am Abend*)."²³ *Le
soir* [the evening] (I add this in Latin, in a Latin language, since
Heidegger doesn't mention this, but it might have interested
him that *le soir, sera* in Italian, supposedly comes from *serus*,
the Latin meaning "late" (*la tarde* in Spanish), *le soir*, the evening, is lateness. It comes from the Sanskrit *sr*: to go, follow,
follow after. Heidegger could have played up this *soir, sera, sr*,
since what it means is precisely the late hour of what comes *am
Abend* and in the *Abendland*, in the Occident.)

Heidegger never, to my knowledge and in his written texts,
praises that which can be said or can only be said in Latin or
French. I've been told that one day he supposedly said,²⁴ in
a somewhat envious tone, "You have a nice word in French,
'*regarder*' [to watch], which has *la garde*, what keeps in view
[*garde en vue*]" (not what keeps in custody [*garde à vue*] but

22. Heidegger, 73.
23. Heidegger, 73.
24. See Martin Heidegger, "Seminar in Zähringen (1973)," in *Seminare*
(*GA* 15), ed. C. Ochwadt (1986; Frankfurt am Main: Vittorio Klostermann,
2005), 118. Published in English as Martin Heidegger, "Seminar in Zähringen 1973," in *Four Seminars*, trans. Andrew Mitchell and François Raffoul
(Bloomington: Indiana University Press, 2012), 68.

what keeps and watches and protects and holds in the look [*regard*]). But no luck for this French word, no luck in any case for Latin, since this word seems to come, if I believe my *Littré*, from the Old High German *warten*, beware, from the root *war*, to consider, to beware, which is found in the German *wahr* (true) and in the Latin *verus, vereor* (to be continued).

So, the step beyond toward the country of the stranger happens *am Abend*. "Therefore the last line of the poem says":[25]

Abend wechselt Sinn und Bild.[26]
. . .
Evening alters sense and image.[27]

It may seem strange that Heidegger concludes from this that the step beyond toward the stranger, toward the country of the stranger happens in the evening, from this verse that says that the evening alters sense and image. It's a bit elliptical. One has to assume that the moment of the passage into the country of the stranger is the moment of a *Wechsel*, a change and mutation of sense and image. But what is a change of sense and image? It would not be possible to respond to this question without getting into a whole meditation on the sense of the word "sense" (as we've seen) and, as for the word *Bild*, without taking into account everything Heidegger says about it elsewhere (*Holzwege*[28]), whether it's a question either of the authority of this motif in modern metaphysics or of the metaphysical rhetoric of the image, of metaphor, and so on. A brief detour here: it will have to do both with the metaphor

25. Heidegger, "Die Sprache im Gedicht," 73.
26. Trakl, "Herbstseele," quoted in Heidegger, 73.
27. Trakl, "Autumn Soul," in *Poems and Prose*, 66/67.
28. Martin Heidegger, "Die Zeit des Weltbildes," in *Holzwege* (*GA* 5), ed. Friedrich-Wilhelm von Herrmann (Frankfurt am Main: Vittorio Klostermann, 1977). Published in English as "The Age of the World Picture," in *Off the Beaten Track*, ed. and trans. Julian Young and Kenneth Haynes (Cambridge: Cambridge University Press, 2002), 57–73.

we are talking about right now and with nearness, this value of nearness we saw a moment ago, the nearness to being or the origin becoming in a way what decided the essence of the human and the history of Europe or the Occident. What does metaphor mean, and what does nearness mean? I pose the question just long enough for a detour—and to refer you to other texts, since I am following as much as I can the rule of a reading of this text on Trakl that is as internal as possible.

The two passages I will evoke both deal, if you will, with neighborhood (*Nachbarschaft*). You'll agree that they must be of interest to us considering that we are interested in "country" and place and nation and habitat, etc. And—another reason for us to take an interest—this neighborhood is first and foremost, in this case, the neighborhood of *Denken* and *Dichten*, thinking and poetry, according to the worn and effaced, effacing association between the two words. The first passage from Heidegger that I would like to read can be found in the lectures titled "*Das Wesen der Sprache*" (translated into French as "*Le déploiment de la parole*" ["The Unfolding of Language"]) in *Unterwegs zur Sprache*:

> Presumably this lies partly in the fact that the two exceptional modes of saying, poetizing and thinking, were not explicitly sought out, that is to say, sought out in their neighborhood. Yet we indeed talk often enough about poetizing and thinking. This phrase has already become trite and an empty formula. Perhaps the "and" in the phrase "poetizing and thinking" receives its fullness and determination if we let ourselves come to the sense that the "and" might mean the neighborhood of poetizing and thinking.
>
> Immediately we will require, however, a clarification of what "neighborhood" is here supposed to mean, and by what right we speak and can speak about such a thing. A neighbor [*Nachbar*], as the word itself tells us, is one who dwells near [*in die Nähe*] to and with another. Thus this other himself becomes the neighbor of the first one.

Neighborhood is therefore a relation resulting from the fact that one draws into the nearness of another. Neighborhood is the result, that is to say, the consequence and effect of one settling next to another. To speak of the neighborhood of poetizing and thinking means, then, that the two of them dwell across from each other, that one has settled across from the other, that one has been drawn into the nearness of the other. This remark on what characterizes neighborhood moves within a metaphorical discourse. Or are we already saying something about the issue itself? What does "metaphorical discourse" mean, then? We readily have recourse to this term, without bearing in mind that we may not appeal to it in a reliable way as long as it remains indeterminate what discourse is, what metaphor is, and the extent to which language speaks in metaphors, if it does speak so at all. We thus leave everything wide open here. Let us keep to what is most urgent, namely, to seek out the neighborhood of poetizing and thinking—that is, now, the across-from-each-other of the two.

Fortunately, we do not need either to search for this neighborhood or to seek it out. We are already abiding in it. We move within it.[29]

The other passage can be found in the same series of lectures, further on:

We would remain stuck in metaphysics if we wished to take as a metaphor this Hölderlinian naming in the phrase "words, like flowers."

[. . .]

We can see this simple relation once we consider anew the extent to which we are everywhere on the way within

---

29. Heidegger, "Das Wesen der Sprache," 175–76; "The Nature of Language," in *On the Way to Language*, 81–82 (translation modified here and below).

the neighborhood of the modes of saying. As such, poetizing and thinking have always been exceptional (*ausgezeichnet*). Their neighborhood did not come to them by chance, from somewhere or other, as though either of them were able, by itself, to be what it is outside their neighborhood. Accordingly, we must experience them within, and on the basis of their neighborhood, that is, on the basis of that which determines neighborhood as such. Neighborhood, it was said, does not first create nearness; rather, nearness appropriates [*ereignet*] neighborhood. Yet what does nearness mean?

As soon as we try to reflect on the matter we have already committed ourselves to a long path of thought. Here, we are now taking just a few steps. They do not lead forward but back, back to where we already are. The steps do not form a sequence in the succession from here to there, except at best in their outward appearance. Rather, they configure themselves into a gathering unto the same and wend their way back to this same. What looks like a detour is a retreat into the proper moving-path [*Be-wëgung*] on the basis of which neighborhood is determined. This is nearness.

When we think of nearness, farness announces itself. Both stand in a certain contrast to each other, as different magnitudes of the distance to objects. The measurement of magnitude is achieved as we calculate stretches in terms of their length or shortness. Thus, the measurements of the lengths so measured are each time taken from a stretch by which, alongside which, the number that measures the magnitude of the stretch is computed. To measure something against something else, by moving alongside it, is called in Greek *parametrein*. The stretches by and alongside which we measure nearness and farness as distances are the succession of "nows," that is, time, and the beside-front-behind-above-below of the points here and there, that is, space. To the calculative representation, space and time appear as parameters for the measurement of nearness and farness, and these in turn as static distances. But space and

time do not serve only as parameters; their essence is immediately depleted in this character—the early forms of which
are discernible early in Western thinking—that was then,
in the course of the modern age, firmly established as the
standard representation by this way of thinking.[30]

I return to the evening that alters sense and image.
If, then, the evening that alters sense and image here determines the country, *das Land*, we are speaking of the Occident, which is called *Abendland*, the country of the evening,
the country not of the delay but of lateness, the country of
lateness or the late-country. "The country towards which the
one who died too soon declines [*untergeht*: *Untergang*, setting sun [*couchant*]] is the country of this evening [and not
the *couchant*, since, as we saw, the Occident is not the *Couchant* for Heidegger and must not be thought in this kind of regional of geophysical way]."[31] The country in which the young
dead man declines, which is the country of the evening, the
country as evening, we saw a bit earlier that it was also, like
every county, the place of a promise (*Versprechen*): the country, *das Land*, is, like every country, what promises dwelling . . . Now, here, what promises the dwelling, toward which
the young dead man does not sink or die but descends, declines, goes down, is the country of the evening, the country as late-country. This lateness promises. Here, having determined what country—promise of dwelling in a free, open
realm (*freien Bereich*)—and evening are, Heidegger has only
to draw our attention to the fact that this country of the evening is named "Occident" by Trakl: "*Die Ortschaft des Ortes*
(Fr. trans.: "*la contrée capable d'un tel site* [!]" ["the region capable of such a site"]) that gathers in itself Trakl's *Gedicht* is the
concealed essence (*das verborgene Wesen*) *der Abgeschiedenheit*

30. Heidegger, "Das Wesen der Sprache," 195–200; "The Nature of Language," 100–102.
31. Heidegger, "Die Sprache im Gedicht," 73.

[of the de-parture, the Dis-cease] and is called '*Abendland*' (Occident)."[32] Clearly, however, to translate *Abendland* as "Occident" reinscribes us in the space from which one must distance oneself.

What is this *Abendland*? Right away, Heidegger distinguishes it from the Platonico-Christian Occident and Europe. But does he distinguish it through some marked characteristic, through a difference or distinction of content? Not at all, it seems to me. It is again a question of the same structure of repetition we have been questioning since last time, a repetition that delves further, toward the more originary, but in order to find there only the thought of what gave birth to that which came about and which, without being conflated with it, is nevertheless nothing other than its possibility—but a possibility that is not an abstract condition of possibility, nor a power, a capacity, a program, or a gene. But what, then? Well, I think one mustn't dissociate the paradox of these repetitions from a value of promise that, in general, is overlooked in Heidegger, but which seems more and more to me to play an essential role that ought to be related rigorously to the thinking of the gift.[33] Here we would have to open a very long parenthesis or a very long detour that would lead us to discuss this discreet but essential role of speech as promise in Heidegger. I will only indicate—that is, promise—this discussion of the promise in Heidegger. I will emphasize first that, to my knowledge, it is something he rarely speaks of by name, no doubt because he thinks that it is implied in other themes he discusses explicitly and copiously (commitment, decision, call, *Ruf*, *heißen*, etc.). Having emphasized that, I believe that an explicit and specific discussion of the promise, by that name, obliges us to take into account, perhaps in a different theoretical context, a structure of speech, notably what is call performative speech, and which

32. Heidegger, 73.
33. Derrida crossed out by hand several interlinear words in the typescript: "*Was heisst Denken?*, hand, oath, performative."

provides one of the privileged examples of utterances known as performative (the performative of a promise). One can easily imagine all the objections Heidegger would have raised against "speech act"[34] theory and, especially, against applying it to his text or the texts he questions. Nonetheless, I believe there would be much to be done and said *between* the two styles of thinking and the two approaches. So, if I were discussing the promise in Heidegger, apart from what I've just recalled (the rarity of allusions to the promise as such in Heidegger and the necessity of passing by way of a problematic of the performative, or even a problematization of speech act theory (see de Man, etc.)), I would say at least two things and give two references.

1. The whole discourse and thinking of the hand (particularly in the passage from *Was heisst Denken?* and the *Parmenides* that we read[35]) can be gathered around the gift *and* the promise, the promise being a gift and the gift (which gives nothing present—to be developed—) a promise. And in the *Parmenides*,[36] in the list of hand gestures that are not reducible to the grasping of the *Greiforgane*, there was the oath (*Schwur*), which is a form of promise.

2. In *Was heisst Denken?*, a particular passage in which Heidegger, in order to ask *was heisst Denken?*—what does thinking mean?, or what is called thinking?—dwells at length on what *heißen* means, what it means to call, as *heißen* in German. This is one of the finest and richest and most necessary moments in this course; I cannot gather or sum it up here, I refer you to it.[37] But in a paragraph explaining what *heißen* means in its originary sense, very near its root, *in seinem angestammten Sagen*, Heidegger notes that *heißen*

34. In English in the original.
35. See Derrida, "Heidegger's Hand (*Geschlecht* II)."
36. Heidegger, *Parmenides*, 118.
37. Interlinear addition: "(. . . 'what does thinking call'? etc.)"; see above, p. xxii, note 26.

means to command, "not in the sense of giving commands and orders [jussive performative!] but in the sense of commending, entrusting, giving into safe-keeping, keeping safely."[38] And he continues: "A promise (*Verheißung*) means (*besagt*): *einen Zuruf zusprechen* (to bring by speaking a call), such that what is said [or spoken, *Gesprochene*] is a commitment (*Zugesagtes*), a word [implicitly, a word that is given, *ein Versprochenes*: a promised thing, something promised]."[39] There are two verbs for promise: *verheißen*, *Verheißung*, and *versprechen*. Heidegger plays on this, without playing.

Die Sprache spricht. De Man: *die Sprache verspricht (sich)* (explain at length).[40]

In the text on Trakl, it is the word *versprechen* that is used to say promising, first that of the country, *das Land* being what promises dwelling, and then—we are getting there—the *Abendland* which, because it is more ancient, being closer to the dawn or the origin (thus also to the dawn of tomorrow, like every twilight) than the Platonic and Christian Occident,

Is more promising ["holds more promise" ["*de meilleure promesse*"], as the French translators are right to translate so as to avoid a "*prometteur*" ["promising"] that has horrible connotations in French, *versprechender*] *als das platonisch-christliche und gar als das europäisch vorgestellte* [not "European ideology" ["*idéologie européenne*"] as the French translation says, but that which is represented in a European fashion, if you will].[41]

38. Heidegger, *Was heisst Denken?*, 122; *What Is Called Thinking?*, 118 (translation modified here and below).

39. Heidegger, *Was heisst Denken?*, 122; *What Is Called Thinking?*, 118.

40. Paul de Man, "Promises," in *Allegories of Reading: Figural Language in Rousseau, Nietzsche, Rilke and Proust* (New Haven, CT: Yale University Press, 1979), 246–77.

41. Heidegger, "Die Sprache im Gedicht," 73.

Thus the *Abendland* named by Trakl (the title of two of his poems) is at once more originary, more matutinal, and consequently more portentous of the future, richer with promise than the European or Platonico-Christian (hyphen: question of the hyphen not posed) Occident. It is, then, like every extreme twilight, closer to the morning to come because it is older than the ancient morning. But can one say that the schema of revolution, the course of the sun, is absent from what Heidegger says? I don't believe so. Draw a circle on the board? . . . [42]

It is a question, then, of thinking this *Abendland* as a promise of the morning, and the *Abgeschiedenheit*, the place of Trakl's *Gedicht*, also as a departure in this sense. A curious thing happens, by the way, in the French translation. I'll read you first the translation of a sentence that says in German: *"Denn die Abgeschiedenheit ist 'Anbeginn' eines steigenden Weltjahres, nicht Abgrund des Verfalls."* "For the Dis-cease is the 'casting off' of an era about to break, not the bottomless abyss of the fall."[43] First of all, to translate *Anbeginn* as *"appareillage"* ["casting off"] when up to this point they were using this same word to translate *Versammlung*, on the pretext that in *Versammlung*, gathering, there is the value of sameness [*pareil*] or of matching [*appareiller*] as one matches a pair of shoes, to translate, then, *Anbeginn* (which means beginning, departure) with the same word, which is now drawn toward the setting sail of a ship, is incredibly frivolous (a bad "play on words" that is out of tune, *pareil/appareil*).

Of course this bad play on words is justified at least to the extent that the moment (which is not a moment *in* time) of *Abgeschiedenheit*, of departure, is also the moment of the place of the *Gedicht*, that is, a moment of gathering. And the whole obvious paradox of this situation (*Erörterung*) is indeed

42. As such in the typescript.
43. The French translation reads: "Car le Dis-cès est 'l'appareillage' d'une ère en voie d'éclore, non l'abîme sans fond de la déchéance."

that, the gathered and gathering sameness of de-parture and of place, of departure as setting off, beginning, initiation and as separation, dislocation on the one hand, of place as gathering on the other hand.

This is why there is nothing negative and thus nothing dialectical (not the Hegelian circle) in this *Abendland* and in this Dis-cease that is not death. There is promise and awaiting (is this so un-Christian, even if it were unphilosophical: question of the hyphen, I already posed the question, I won't go back to it; one can imagine Christians or Judeo-Christians easily appropriating this somewhat messianic, if not eschatological thinking). Now, to conclude, I will translate the paragraph that follows in order to pick up on a word and make a brief digression. This word is once again the word "passage" as *Übergang*, transgression, step beyond. Here it is:

> The Occident (*Abendland*) latent [concealed: *verborgene*] in the Dis-cease [departure, *Abgeschiedenheit*] does not sink (*geht nicht unter*: no *Untergang, couchant,* or sinking ship) but remains [*bleibt*: stays], insofar as it awaits (*wartet*) its dwellers (*Bewohner*) as the country of the decline (*als das Land des Untergangs*) into spiritual night. The country of decline (*das Land des Untergangs*) is a passage [transition, or transgression, *Übergang*] into the beginning [toward the beginning: *in den Anfang*] of a morning [of precociousness, of what comes early, *der Frühe*] that is concealed within it (*in ihm verborgenen*).[44]

This *Übergang*, like *Überschritt* above (step beyond, transgression, passage over), given that it is the passage beyond the human of the philosophico-Christian Occident, is also the passage beyond the human of humanism and so-called Western reason. Beyond, at the same time, the humanism-cosmopolitanism pair, or the nationalism/internationalism, nationalism/abstract

44. Heidegger, "Die Sprache im Gedicht," 73.

universalism opposition that amount to the same thing and are both caught up in the same system, let's say the same day, a day that is too short, that began too late and finished too early. This seems to me to echo—and this is the note I'll conclude on today—what is said about the Nietzschean overman, about the human as *animal rationale* and the beast in another passage from *Was heisst Denken?*. I will bring this all together under the heading "question of reason" (in German *Vernunft*, which Heidegger brings into play with *vernehmen*: to grasp, apprehend, comprehend, take, understand). It is the grasping of the beast, who has no hands but only prehensile organs (*Greiforgane*)—or concepts. This passage can be found: *Was heisst Denken?* It has to do with Nietzsche, the overman, *Übermensch*, and the triple question of knowing what the *über* (trans, meta) means in: "1. The *Übergehen*; 2. Whence the *Übergang* departs (*von wo weg der Übergang geht*); 3. Whither (*wohin*) the *Übergang geschieht* (happens)."[45]

(Reference to Nietzsche and the essence of the human not yet *fest gestellt* in the text on Trakl.[46])

Read *Was heisst Denken?* in French and comment.

The overman goes beyond, overpasses today's—therefore, the last—man. Man, when he does not stop at today's kind of human, is a passage, a transition; he is a bridge; he is "a rope strung between the animal and the overman." The overman, strictly understood, is the figure and form of man to which he who passes over is passing over. Zarathustra is not yet the overman himself, but only the very first to be passing over to him—he is the overman in the process of becoming. For various reaons, we limit our reflections here to this preliminary figure of the overman. But we must first give heed to the passage across. Next, we must give closer thought to the second point, the site of departure of him

45. Heidegger, *Was heisst Denken?*, 64; *What Is Called Thinking?*, 60.
46. Heidegger, "Die Sprache im Gedicht," 41.

who crosses over—that is, how matters stand with today's man, the last man. And third, we must give thought to where he goes who passes across, that is, what stance man comes to take as he passes across.

The first point, the passage across, will become clear to us only as we give thought to the second and third points, the whence and the whither of the man who passes over and who, in passing over, is transformed.

The man whom the man who is passing over goes beyond and away from is today's man. To remind us of that man's essential definition, Nietzsche calls him the animal that has not yet been firmly secured [*fest-gestellte*]. This implies: *homo est animal rationale*. "Animal" does not yet mean just any living being; a plant is also a living being, yet we cannot call man a rational vegetable. "Animal" means beast; *animaliter* means (for example in Saint Augusine, as well) "bestially." Man is the rational beast. Reason [*Vernunft*] is the grasping [*Vernehmen*] of what is, which always means also what can be and ought to be. To grasp implies, in ascending order: to welcome and take in; to accept and take in the encounter; to take up face to face; to undertake and see through—and this means to talk through. The Latin for talking through is *reor*; the Greek *reo* (as in rhetoric) is the ability to take up something and see it through; *reri* is *ratio*; *animal rationale* is the animal which lives by grasping what is, in the manner described. The grasping that prevails within reason produces and adduces purposes, establishes rules, provides means and ways, and attunes reason to the modes of action. The grasping of reason unfolds as this manifold providing [*Stellen*], which is first of all and always a setting-forth [*Vor-stellen*]. Thus one might also say: *homo est animal rationale*—man is the animal that sets-forth. A mere animal, such as a dog, never represents anything [*stellt nie etwas vor*], it can never set anything before *itself* [*vor*-sich-*stellen*]; to do so, the animal would have to grasp *itself*. It cannot say "I," it cannot talk at all. By contrast man, according to metaphysical doctrine, is the representing animal which has the property that it can speak. Upon this essential definition—which is, however, never thought through more fully to its roots—there is then constructed the doctrine of man as the person, which doctrine can thereafter be expressed theologically. *Persona* means the actor's mask through which his dramatic tale is sounded. Insofar as man, as the one who grasps, grasps what is, we can think of him as the *persona*, the mask, of Being.[47]

47. Heidegger, *Was heisst Denken?*, 64–66; *What Is Called Thinking?*, 60–62 (translation modified).

[118] *Geschlecht III*

Twelfth Session

We talked—I won't return to it—about the "country," the *das Land*, and analyzed the paradoxes of a certain circle of what one could call, in a language that is not at all Heidegger's own, revolutionary promise. Heidegger, for that matter, does not even speak of a circle in this passage, fearing that it might be reappropriated by a Hegelian type of thinking. But he does speak of the promise twice, which I dwelled on. Revolutionary promise in the sense of the revolution of the day or the year, the more matutinal, thus the more ancient, remaining more promising than the less matutinal. In the evening, *am Abendland*, in the country of the evening, what declines toward the more matutinal promises more than what, like the Platonico-Christian Occident, is not old enough, not matutinal enough. We also followed the path of the *Übergang* and the *Überschritt*, of the step beyond toward the country of the stranger or toward the beginning that is still concealed in the country of the Occident. And we followed this *Über-gang* or *Schritt* all the way to the vicinity of *Was heisst Denken?*, where Heidegger evokes Nietzsche's *Übermensch*, which goes beyond the animal, the beast, and the *animal rationale* as the animal of grasping, taking, understanding reason, with the passage that links *Vernunft* to *vernehmen* (to grasp, take, understand, conceive, etc.). A discourse on the human of grasping reason which is, to be sure, the old human, yet a human who is at the same time not old enough, thus not young enough, no longer to come, without a future.

Today we find, still in this third part of the text on Trakl, at the quasi closing of the circle, the interpretation of the "*Ein*" of "Ein *Geschlecht*" that we discussed paraliptically at the outset. The entire lexicon of the blow, stamp, or strike (*Schlag*) gets mobilized there, and we will have more trouble than ever in translating.

Heidegger has just suggested that the departure (*Abgeschiedenheit*) in which the *Abendland* conceals itself does not sink but awaits its dwellers as a country of promise, every country being that which promises dwelling. At that moment, as if he were just stumbling upon it without having paved the way, Heidegger asks: "May we talk about a coincidence (*Zufall*) [. . .], that of two Trakl poems explicitly name the *Abendland*?" and even in their very title. One is titled "Abendland"—Heidegger cites the title but nothing else, not even recalling that there are four versions of it and that it belongs to *Gesang des Abgeschiedenen*; the other, which Heidegger quotes, is called "Abendländisches Lied" (in the collection *Siebengesang des Todes*).[1] Heidegger declares, without any further clarification, that it "sings the same thing as '*Gesang des Abgeschiedenen*,'" the title in quotation marks in his text, a reference to the collection in which the other poem is found—the French translation skips over the quotation marks, as if it weren't a title (of a poem and a collection), and thus becomes more or less unintelligible here. Without any further precaution, Heidegger will quote only three lines from this poem, the first and a part of the penultimate. He is interested in nothing else in the poem, neither its composition, nor the different figures that are formed or displaced there, nothing else. What links these two lines, this line and the portion of this other line, what links them, which Heidegger wants to bring to light, abandoning the rest to darkness, is, on the one hand, the passage—let's call it semantic—between

1. See Trakl, "Song of the Western World," in *Poems and Prose*, 76/77.

a certain blow (*Schlag*) in one compound word (*Flügelschlag*) and *Geschlecht*, where, this time, *Schlag* itself gets inserted in a composite. This passage is totally effaced by the French translation. On the other hand, in a strange gesture that one can recognize only (and it took me a certain amount of time to notice it) if one returns to the poem as a whole, Heidegger exploits the punctuation of the poem rather audaciously. Let me try to explain. It is a question—let's take note of this, since what interests us in all of this is a certain thinking of the two, of difference as duality and play between multiple dualities, the two at least two times (we already saw, as you'll remember, *Zweideutigkeit*, then a double ambiguity, two times two senses)—it is a question here, then, let's take note of it, of a colon [*deux points*, literally "two points"—Trans.] two times, a double *Doppelpunkt*. There is a first one after the first line, and then "*ein zweiter Doppelpunkt*"[2] on the threshold of the penultimate line.

The first line, says Heidegger, is a call (*Ruf*), a call that is *sich neigend*, that bends down, perhaps in greeting, a "*salutation*" ["greeting"] says the French translation, *staunend*, in an astonished or astonishing way, "*extasiée*" ["in extasy"] says the French translation.[3]

This line is (I quoted it at the very beginning[4]):

> O der Seele nächtlicher Flügelschlag:[5]
> . . .
> O the soul's nocturnal wing-beat:[6]

The first colon leaves this "beat" [*coup*], this *Schlag*, suspended. How does Heidegger interpret this colon, this first colon? He thinks that what follows—namely, the entire poem, in other

---

2. Heidegger, "Die Sprache im Gedicht," 74.

3. Heidegger, 74.

4. See Derrida, *Psyche*, 2:55.

5. Trakl, "Abendländisches Lied," quoted in Heidegger, "Die Sprache im Gedicht," 74.

6. Trakl, "Song of the Western World," in *Poems and Prose*, 76/77.

words four stanzas or twenty-two lines of verse, or in any case twenty lines until the appearance of the other, second colon—is the explanation included under the banner, as it were, of this colon. Now, the other stanzas also include periods, commas, and semicolons. But, for Heidegger, everything that follows the first colon and the *Schlag* of *Flügelschlag* comes to answer this *Schlag*, to define it, complete it, describe it, like a suspended flight, as that which maintains this wing-beat until the appearance, after the twentieth line, of a second *Doppelpunkt* before the "*Ein Geschlecht*" that will answer, as it were, the initial "wing-beat" (*Flügelschlag*).

Board:
O der Seele nächtlicher Flügelschlag:

20 verses
. . . . :
Ein Geschlecht . . .

Heidegger quotes nothing else, he quotes nothing of the twenty lines or the last two, he doesn't even quote the line in which the second colon is found:

Aber strahlend heben die silbernen Lider die Liebenden:
. . .
Yet radiantly the silver songs raise the lovers:[7]

---

7. Trakl, "Song of the Western World," in *Poems and Prose*, 78/79. The German word "*Lider*" that Derrida here translates into French as "*chants*" ["songs"] (no doubt due to the homophony with "*Lieder*") means rather "eyelids."
For "lovers," Derrida gives in French both the usual word "*amant*" and the more unusual "*aimant*," which is the present participle of the verb *aimer* (to love) but also the word for "magnet," thus recalling what he says earlier of Heidegger's essay on Trakl, namely, that it "magnetized" [*aimanté*] his reading of Heidegger and *Geschlecht* from the beginning. (—Trans.)

If Heidegger avoids quoting or elucidating (*erläutern*) all of the poem in the space between the two colons, this is because he deems it obvious that the entire poem, titled "Occidental Song," describes the passing from sunrise to sunset, the course of the sun and the seasons, of the year from Orient to Occident; here again the French translation has to efface with three words the three words with which Heidegger designates the remainder of the poem. The French translation says:

> [. . .] what follows [in the poem, what follows the first colon] is comprised in the same whole up until the passage from the decline into a rising [where Heidegger writes: *Der Vers endet mit einem Doppelpunkt, der alles ihm Folgende einschließt bis zum Übergang aus dem Untergang in den Aufgang*].[8]

The *Gang* is the year (*Jahr*), that which goes, you remember (comment . . .).[9] And it is indeed, we can check this even though Heidegger does not quote it, in the last stanza after the previous stanza had named the "repose of the evening" (*Ruh des Abends*), three verses after "*O, die bittere Stunde des Untergangs*," that the song exalts or raises up the lovers and after the word "*Liebenden*," we find the second *Doppelpunkt*. It is in this place in the poem, after the evening, *Untergang*, thus at sunrise (*Aufgang*) as Heidegger supposes, that we once again find a colon, and after the colon the simple word ("*ihm folgt das einfache Wort*"), these very simple words that will say the simple, the one: "'Ein *Geschlecht*.' The 'one' (*Ein*) [Heidegger notes] is emphasized."[10] "Emphasized" is "*betont*"; this is important, because it is what will allow Heidegger to declare that this emphasis, as a marked intonation, is an emphasis in the song,

8. Heidegger, "Die Sprache im Gedicht," 74.
9. See above, p. 38.
10. Heidegger, 74.

and you'll recall that Heidegger says the poem must be sung—moreover, it bears the word "*Lied*" in its title, and before the colon the verse names "*die silbernen Lider*"[11]; this emphasis as marked intonation gives the *Grundton*, the fundamental tone of the poem, and not only of this poem but of Trakl's silent *Gedicht*, his proper place. This proper place is the *Ein*, the marked intonation of the *Ein* in the syntagm "Ein *Geschlecht*."

Heidegger uses as grounds for his argument, or rather reinforces his argument with the fact that, to his knowledge, this is the only underscored word in all of Trakl's poetic oeuvre.[12] Since obviously the printed word is not underscored, but what we call underscoring here in this case is not, in typographical terms, the passage to italics, as it often is, but a supplementary spacing, Heidegger literally writes not "the only word written in italics," as the French translation says, but: "*Es ist, soweit ich sehe, das einzige gesperrt geschriebene Wort in den Dichtungen Trakls.*"[13] *Sperren*, in the code of typography, is to space. After this second colon, the "*Ein*" of "Ein *Geschlecht*" would come not only to answer the first *Flügelschlag*, the wing-beat suspended by the first colon, but to give, because it is *betont*, the fundamental tone of the *Gedicht*—and not only of this *Gedicht*, as place of this poem, but of the whole of Trakl's *Gedicht*. This may seem exorbitant, as a glance [*coup d'œil*] (*Blicksprung*), as an interpretative leap in a wing-beat [*coup d'aile*]. There are an impressive wing-beat and glance here. But recall that, at the beginning of the text, Heidegger was justifying the necessity and risk of the blow [*coup*], of the leap, of the glance (*Blicksprung*).[14] Heidegger does not say, for that matter, that the "*Ein*" of "Ein *Geschlecht*" is the fundamental intonation but that it conceals in itself, it reserves, it hides or holds (*birgt*) the *Grundton*. And this *Grundton* that is concealed in a word, that

11. On the confusion here between "*Lider*" and "*Lieder*," see p. 122, note 7.

12. Heidegger, 74.

13. Heidegger, 74. "It is, as far as I see, the only spaced-out written word in Trakl's poems." (—Trans.)

14. See above, p. 15.

is sheltered there, without being said, then, without phenom-
enalizing itself, like an intonation in itself inaudible, or audible
only through and beyond marked intonations, this *Grundton* is
that "from which the *Gedicht* of this *Dichter* [singular] silences
the secret (*das Geheimnis schweigt*)."[15] By saying "remains tacit"
["*demeure tacite*"] here ("the Poet's Dict remains tacit" ["*le Dict
du Poète demeure tacite*"]), the French translation misses the
transitivity of the *Schweigen* that will specifically be in question, on two occasions in a moment, and which is specifically
marked here: the *Gedicht* silences the *Geheimnis*, the secret as
what is in the household, at home, *heim*, etc. The *Gedicht* is
not only silent, one may say that it silences, actively, or in any
case transitively. On the next page, Heidegger will twice insist
on the transitive character, first of the verb *schweigen* in a Trakl
verse, "*Es schweigt die Seele den blauen Frühling*" ['the soul silences the blue springtime'—the French translation does not
begin with the "in truth" in order to mark the inversion],"[16] and
then of the word "*sprach*" in "Kaspar Hauser Lied":

> Gott sprach eine sanfte Flamme zu seinem Herzen:
> O Mensch![17]
> . . .
> God spoke a gentle flame to his heart:
> O Man![18]

What, then, is the unity of this *Ein* that is thus silenced by
the *Gedicht*? The unity of this *Geschlecht*:

> The unity of the *one Geschlecht* (*Die Einheit des* einen *Ge-
> schlechtes*) *entquillt dem Schlag* [emerges, springs from the
> *Schlag*, "from the stock" ["*de la souche*"] says the French

15. Heidegger, 74.
16. Trakl, "Im Dunkel," quoted in Heidegger, 75; "In the Dark," in *Poems
and Prose*, 100/101.
17. Trakl, "Kaspar Hauser Lied," quoted in Heidegger, 75.
18. Trakl, "Kaspar Hauser Song," in *Poems and Prose*, 54/55.

translation, to be sure, but also the strike—from what strike, from the strike] that, from out of departedness (*der aus der Abgeschiedenheit her*) and the quieter quietude that prevails in it [in the departure: *aus der in ihr waltenden stilleren Stille*], from out of its "legends of the forest" [in quotation marks that are omitted in the French translation, "*Sagen des Waldes*": "saying of the forest"], from its "measure and law" ["*Maß und Gesetz*," again between omitted quotation marks: a quotation but not from this poem] through "the lunar paths of the departed one" [again quotation marks omitted,[19] a quotation from another poem: *durch "die mondenen Pfade der Abgeschiedenen,"* so, the strike that] gathers (*versammelt*) the *Zwietracht der Geschlechter* [the discord of the sexes or genera] simply [in a simple way, *einfältig*] unto the more gentle (*sanftere*) twofold.[20]

The strike, or the stock, *der Schlag*, is thus what gathers (and thus constitutes place), what gathers simply, in simplicity (*einfältig*), discord (agonistic duality) into gentle and tender duality. The strike gathers the *Zwietracht* into *Zwiefalt*. It is, then, the strike, it strikes between two times two, two dualities or differences of *Geschlecht*—two sexual differences, but which are not sexual only, and the meaning of sexuality here is enveloped in the polysemy of *Geschlecht*; it is perhaps when it is separated from this polysemy and determined only as sexual that the *Zwietracht* appears, along with the war of the sexes. It is this simplicity and this gentleness of difference that announces itself as the future or the very ancient in departure or dis-cease, beyond the Platonico-Christian Occident. This gentle difference, insofar as it stems from one strike, or likewise from a stock insofar as it is a stamp.[21] This stamp strikes the

19. The 1976 French edition that Derrida used indeed omits almost all the quotation marks of this type; the later edition of 1981 happily restored them.

20. Heidegger, "Die Sprache im Gedicht," 74.

21. As such in the typescript.

[126] *Geschlecht III*

one, the unity of the one in the two—and we will see that the one is not opposed to the two, in truth it is not even distinguished from it. We must also say, even though this is not what Heidegger says explicitly, that this strike of the one in *Geschlecht* is also the strike of the word that gathers into the one and into the gathering unity of the word "*Geschlecht*" this multiplicity of significations, all the blows of which come in one single mark, one single word, a word that also says gathering (*Ge-*), in order to seal their consonance. In the middle of the next paragraph, Heidegger stresses that the word "*Geschlecht*" thus keeps "*seine volle bereits gennante mehrfältige Bedeutung* (its aforementioned full manifold meaning)."[22] "The 'one' in the expression 'Ein *Geschlecht*' does not mean '*eins*' instead of two."[23] This is not an arithmetic designation. The latter designates objects, discrete series that are *vorhanden*, objects close at hand. *Geschlecht*, we will say without referring here to any explicit remark of Heidegger's, is not an object, a countable *vorhanden* being. It is more originary than this objectivity. The one and the two are not opposed in it. If one wanted to unfold not only the logic or ontology but the deconstruction of classical—Platonico-Christian—logic and ontology implied by the entire text, one ought to say that this objectifying countability is the effect, precisely, of a privilege granted by Western metaphysics which has privileged the form of the *vorhanden* being (substance, object, subject) that lends itself to countability and mathematization, and in doing so has concealed something of *Geschlecht* and the gentle difference . . .

If the "one" of "Ein *Geschlecht*" cannot say one instead of two, "it also does not mean the monotony [homogeneity, *Einerlei*] of a bland sameness [*einer faden Gleichheit*, undifferentiated equality]."[24] But it is still necessary to specify—and this ressembles, at least, a kind of negative theology of *Geschlecht* that can

22. Heidegger, 74.
23. Heidegger, 74.
24. Heidegger, 74.

be reached only by successively denying, by demarcating every predication; it is, moreover, the judgment "S is P," the attribution of this logic that is in question here: *Geschlecht* is neither this nor that—it is still necessary, then, to specify, negatively, that the "*Ein*" of "Ein *Geschlecht*" is not "unisexuality or same-sexness (*Eingeschlechtlichkeit* or *Gleichgeschlechtlichkeit*)."[25] Here we are not in the mythology of androgyny or hermaphroditism, we are not within the archaizing regression toward two sexes into one, but, if one follows at least the intention of this text, this negative specification, we are within a completely other experience of sexual difference. What's more, this unity of the one is not given, is not a fact or a given, it is a movement, a motion, one could almost say a desire if this word, which Heidegger does not use, were not too heavy here with connotations that have to be handled with caution. There is not the one or the unity of the one, there is the unifying movement, and this unifying movement itself is not phenomenalized, it is concealed, it is sheltered and, moreover, it is silenced by the *Gedicht*. Heidegger writes in a sentence that is also mistreated by the French translation:

> In the emphasized (*betonten*) "*one Geschlecht*" lies concealed (*verbirgt sich*) that which unifies [*jenes Einende*: and not "this unity" ["*cette unité*"] as the French translation has it], that which unites (*einigt*) from out of the gathering [and not "matching" ["*appareillant*"]] blueness of the spiritual night. The phrase [here the whole expression "Ein *Geschlecht*"] speaks from the song [thus from the marked intonation, the accentuation: accent is the song in speech] in which the land of the evening is sung (*worin das Land des Abends gesungen wird*). Accordingly, the word "*Geschlecht*" retains here its aforementioned full manifold meaning. It names first the historical *Geschlecht* of humans, humanity (*das geschichtliche Geschlecht des Menschen, die Menschheit*), as distinct

25. Heidegger, 74.

from other living beings (plants and animals). The word "*Geschlecht*" names then the *Geschlechter* [generations], the stocks, clans, and families of this *Menschengeschlechtes*. The word "*Geschlecht*" names at the same time and everywhere (*zugleich überall*) the *Zwiefalt der Geschlechter*.[26]

We must indeed insist on the singularity of this gesture and this *Ein*. That which unifies, which stems from the singularity of this blow (*Schlag*), or this strike, that which unifies gives rise to a simplicity that is nothing other than duplicity, or a simple duplicity. There is no longer or, rather, there was not nor will there be, there will not have been any opposition between the *Zwiefalt* and the *Einfalt* when the movement has come to the end of its course, at the end of the spiritual night. In the previous paragraph, *einfältig* (simply, in a single fold) was an adverb. In the following paragraph it's a noun. In the previous paragraph, "the strike gathers [Heidegger said] the discord (*Zwietracht*) of the sexes simply (*einfältig*) unto the more gentle [more serene] twofold [*Zwiefalt*: the double fold]."[27] In the following paragraph, "the strike [says Heidegger, *der Schlag*] that stamps the *Geschlechter* into the simplicity of 'Einen *Geschlechts*' (*in die Einfalt des* 'Einen *Geschlechts*') [. . .]."[28]

What does this strike, this blow do? *Der Schlag schlägt*, this strike strikes, says Heidegger, and what resembles—in keeping, precisely, with a gesture typical of Heidegger—a tautology also signifies, more profoundly, that we are dealing here with the signification of that which cannot leave room for a metalanguage, which cannot let itself be defined by anything other than itself, except if the signification to be defined was introduced into the defining signification. Every predication concerning *Schlag* presupposes some *schlagen*, it must be struck, imprinted, it presupposes the blow, just as every definition of

26. Heidegger, 74–75.
27. Heidegger, 74.
28. Heidegger, 75.

Sprache presupposes language enough that one cannot say language is or does this or that, since these values of being and oing are inadequate insofar as they presuppose the *Sprache*: one must therefore say *die Sprache spricht, das Ereignis ereignet, der Schlag schlägt*. These significations cannot be derivative. But how does the strike strike? I will note three things:

1. The strike, contrary to what one might automatically imagine, does not come to sign or seal, if a signature or a seal closes, concludes, contains. Here the strike is, on the contrary, an opening and a path-breaking [*frayage*], its violence or at least its force works as the piercing of a path, the path-breaking, that is to say the break, the breaking in toward a perspective and a passage, a way or a *Weg*. It is, then, a liberation (this is not Heidegger's word) that offers and opens a path where there was none, or no longer one.

    The *Schlag* [. . .] *schlägt* [says the same paragraph] insofar as it lets the soul strike [difficult to translate, the French translation says "strikes the soul open for the path of the blue spring"²⁹] a path [*einschlagen läßt*: *Weg einschlagen* is to set out on a path, the *Schlag* starts the soul on the path by striking it, it sets the soul, in one blow, on the path, it imprints in the soul the movement or the path] toward the "blue spring" (*den Weg in den "blauen Frühling"*), etc.³⁰

    In any event, the blow opens the path, it does not fix into a stamp or type. And this can be said only in the idiom that signs this entire discourse (*Schlag* and the idiomatic expression that links it to *Weg*: untranslatable).
2. Even if this open, broken path (*via rupta*: route, breaking in, etc.) is opened onto the future, onto the springtime or

---

29. The French translation reads: "frappe l'âme d'ouverture pour le chemin du bleu printemps."
30. Heidegger, 75.

morning to come, it remains a path of return. The return means, according to the very problematic figure of the circle I spoke of last time, that the more matutinal, whose promise is most open to the future, is what gives way to the more ancient, the more matutinal of the night before [*la veille*]. "*La veille*" is a good word here for gathering together, in French, all these meanings: *veiller* [to watch over] in the sense of to keep and keep sheltered, vigilance and the watch over the night before [*la veille sur la veille*], over what happened yesterday, the more matutinal of yesterday morning, the evening being now, in the country of the evening, the place or the moment where one watches over what awaits us and is promised us tomorrow, on the eve of which we are. The return means, then, this relation between *veilles*. And the idea of gathering, of the blow that gathers and discord unto the gentle twofold in the simple, this gathering is also a re-assembling that delivers the return to childhood, to early childhood, the more ancient and younger childhood. The sentence that says "the strike (*Schlag*), that stamps *the* Geschlechter into the simplicity of 'Einen *Geschlechts*' [. . .] insofar as it lets the soul strike a path toward the 'blue spring,'" this sentence says that "the strike brings the stocks of the human *Geschlecht* [. . .] back [*zurückbringt*: carries back, brings back home, returns] into the gentleness of quieter childhood."

3. This value of return, of gathering in return, allows us perhaps to see more concretely the link between this reading of Heidegger and our problematic: philosophical nationality and nationalism, supposing that this link is not or no longer overly obvious. Of course, in all of this it is not a question of the nation in the strict and everyday sense, and Heidegger would protest very strongly against this reduction. He would quickly show that the concept of nation and the nationalist claim alike are dependent on a metaphysics in which the theme of *Geschlecht* is not thought in a sufficiently originary way, dependent on a degradation

of the decomposed humanity, precisely, which, because it has lost its "*Heimat,*" wanders between the two symmetrical, antagonistic but indissociable poles of cosmopolitanism and nationalism, these two having in common the same uprootedness with respect to *Sprache*, and so on.

And yet, without rejecting this Heideggerian objection at its level, we must persist in recognizing, in this very denial and this very height, a typically nationalist posture, or at the very least one that guarantees the ultimate foundation of every nationalism. This schema of return is the theme on the basis of which is typically determined, I won't say nationalism, every nationalism, all of nationalism, but it's a word—the word "*Heimkunft*"—without which it is difficult to imagine a nationalism. One could pursue this very far; I don't have the time or, in truth, the desire to go looking here for examples and describe them in detail from this point of view, but I think it would be easy. This return as return to the source [*ressourcement*] can be a withdrawal or the preparation for a new morning or a new leap. Moreover, the line of this nationalist circle can—and this isn't contradictory, we have a model of it in the other form of path that Heidegger describes here— can compose or alternate with another line, that of the journey, the path open toward adventure, path-breaking, what strikes open a new *via rupta*, a new route for a new dwelling, and there, in the dependency or movement of this other line, we have, instead of nostalgic withdrawal toward the originary dwelling, colonial expansion, the future as the adventure of culture or of colonization, of the dwelling that is cultivated and colonized starting from new routes.

If I have the feeling that this sojourn with Heidegger's text does not make us stray from the problematic of philosophical nationalism, this is not only due to the themes, motifs, let's say the content that we are discussing.

I am attempting this reading, as you see, with some difficulty, difficulty in getting across, in translating a language and writing that resist this so well in the French language, to be sure—and often it is the French language that must be transported, translated into Heidegger's German—but difficulties also in translating such a text and such a thinking into a pedagogical discourse or, in any case, the discourse of a seminar. The difficulty would already be different if I were trying this out with a Heidegger seminar in German. This text on Trakl has a mode, a type of process, a manner of advancing that does not always respond to the norms and style that in general regulate Heidegger's seminar. This stems also—not only, but also—from the fact that the text is a *Gespräch* with a poet.

What I've been asking myself the whole time I've been doing this is the following: where would one find, or would one ever find, in another language, in another national philosophical tradition, a philosopher who is also a great university professor of philosophy proceeding in this way, treating language in this way, entering into a *Gespräch* with a poet and with poems that are more or less contemporary, and which belong to his national language? Could you find analogous examples in Greek? No, not to my knowledge. In Latin? No, not to my knowledge. In English or Anglo-American? No, not to my knowledge. In French? If there are any in French, we'd have to see, it's in an entirely different style, and I believe that you would pick up there traces of Heidegger's passage, if not the Heideggerian model.

Consequently, to ask these questions, to undertake these imaginary variations, to experience in doing so this idiomaticity of the Heideggerian gesture, is to reveal national differences and, in fact, practically, through practice, to treat the question of nationalism. Why is it that what Heidegger does has never been done in another language and national tradition? Where does that come from? What does it have to do with? In order to refine these questions, it is necessary to point out that Heidegger is not thinking here simply as a philosopher, but beyond philosophy, questioning philosophy, precisely; it is also necessary to point out that this interrogation is not content to cite a poet or invoke poetic testimony. It defines or presupposes at the same time the definition of a *Gespräch*, of an essential *Zwiesprache* between thinker and poet, both conversing at the same height, as it were (two "peaks"), about the essence of *Sprache* (untranslatable word). This *Gespräch*, its possibility, its definition, its expectation, its situation, are absolutely impossible, ignored, forbidden, or rejected everywhere else, everywhere outside of Germany and perhaps even everywhere in a Germany of today. We could, during the discussion for which I'll reserve some time today and next time, try to imagine together the form, gesture, style, and argumentation that could support this exclusion and this impossibility in the national zones I just mentioned: Greece, Latinity, France, England, the US, but also other national zones we could think of, there are many and more original ones from this perspective. I don't mean to say that this possibility is Heidegger's invention, even though, in a way, it remains to my knowledge absolutely unique and passes by way of a unique signature. But this uniqueness itself would not have been possible without a tradition or a memory, without the presence of a certain type of *Dichten* in the language and history of Germany, without Hölderlin or Trakl, for example.

If one takes this uniqueness into account, the uniqueness that gathers the uniqueness named or signed Heidegger and the uniqueness named "the German language," Hölderlin's or Trakl's *Gedicht*, that is, a certain German poeticity, a sequence at least, plus what one calls "Germany" in general, what we have is a singularity that, however one defines it, has an essential and indissociable relation—itself unique—with, for example, what is said in this text about the country (*Land*), *Geschlecht*, the Occident, etc. (I won't go back over everything.) What the text nods to and opens itself toward, what it calls, cannot be separated from this German possibility—not the possibility of Germany in general, but a possibility that is unthinkable without the destiny of something like the German language and German poeticity, and its relation, its *Gespräch*, with thinking, if not with philosophy.

Is it improper to say that, at least implicitly, everything that is called by Trakl's *Gedicht*, such as Heidegger understands and translates it, passes by way of this uniqueness from which German (the language inseparable from this *Gedicht* and this *Denken*) is indissociable<?> If what I'm saying is acceptable— and we can discuss this—then in the passage that I am about to read, translate, and comment on, one can inscribe this German [*cet Allemand*] each time Heidegger names the country of the evening and the "unique call for the event of the right strike (*nach dem Ereignis des rechten Schlages*)."[31] Immediately after having said that "the strike [. . .] strikes insofar as it lets the soul strike a path toward the 'blue spring,'" Heidegger continues: "The soul sings the path toward the 'blue spring' (*ihn singt die Seele*) *indem sie ihn schweigt* (insofar as it silences it)."[32] Here silence traverses song, and it is even insofar as the song sings that it keeps silent, that it speaks while keeping silent. An equivalence of singing and keeping silent, the song being the present essence, as it were, presence itself, the purest presence, the phenomenon *par excellence* of the poem. But here it is a silencing, not a keeping silent, but a silencing of something. And since it is a question of the blue spring, Heidegger quotes, in order to illustrate this transitive character of the silencing (*schweigen*) that is related, that has a determined relation to what it silences, Heidegger quotes "Im Dunkel" ("In Darkness"):

> Es schweigt die Seele den blauen Frühling.[33]
> . . .
> The soul silences the blue spring.[34]

31. Heidegger, 75.
32. Heidegger, 75.
33. Trakl, "Im Dunkel," quoted in Heidegger, "Die Sprache im Gedicht," 75.
34. Trakl, "In the Dark," in *Poems and Prose*, 100/101.

And in a symmetrical way, he will quote one, two lines from "Kaspar Hauser Lied" in which it is speak/spoke (*sprach*) which, in an apparently equally unusual and ungrammatical way, has a transitive value. But before quoting these two lines from "Kaspar Hauser Lied," he translates, as it were, the silence of "*Es schweigt die Seele den blauen Frühling.*" What does this silence silence, what does it relate to properly? In other words, if silence resonates, as it were, as song, what does this silence sing? Well, this is where *das Land des Abends* (the country of the evening)—which must not be confused with Europe or the Platonico-Christian Occident—which is the very thing that Trakl sings, must be conflated with, or in any case be called something like the German, understood [*entendu*] as the language and the country without which this call would not resonate.

> Trakl's poetry sings *das Land des Abends* (the land of the evening). It (*die Dichtung*) is a unique call (*ein einiges Rufen*) for the appropriative event [the event: *nach dem Ereignis*] of the right strike (*des rechten Schlages*), which speaks [the French translation strangely says "*transfigure*" ["transfigures"] for "*spricht*"] the flame of spirit into gentleness (*der die Flamme des Geistes ins Sanfte spricht*).[35]

One must say, then, that the right strike speaks (transitively) and transforms or transfigures the flame of spirit (which can be Evil, as we've seen) into gentleness, into peace, *ins Sanfte*, still the same word. And this is what Trakl's poetry sings when it sings the country of the evening, it sings this *Sprache* that strikes and in striking right brings peace, gentleness. Is it excessive to claim that this right strike, insofar as it speaks and calls gentleness, has an essential relation with the possibility of language, the German language, in which this is said; and thus that the country of the evening (which is not the Occi-

35. Heidegger, 75.

dent) which Trakl's poetry sings has an essential relation with this *Sprache*; and thus that a certain Germany—not the *de facto* national Germany, etc. (you are now familiar with all these distinctions)—is the place of this call of the Occident beyond the Occident, of the country of the evening beyond the metaphysico-Christian European Occident: the Germany that is called as much as it is the place of the call? Germany as what is silenced by this silent speech, as what is sung? And thus as the place of coming, of event and appropriation (*Ereignis*) of this "Ein *Geschlecht*" which will not take long to be re-named after this recalling of the "right strike" (*rechter Schlag*). Let's look at this to conclude today. To illustrate this transitivity of the *sprechen*, Heidegger thus quotes "Kaspar Hauser Lied": "*Gott sprach eine sanfte Flamme zu seinem Herzen: / O Mensch!*"[36] Transitive speech, speech that not only says something (in principle one does not "speak" something, one speaks, but one "says" something), speech that is transitive not only insofar as it says something but insofar as it does something, insofar as it transforms, transports, transfigures the flame of spirit into gentleness, of the holy flame in or toward or to its heart. A speech, I would say, that is more performative than transitive, or transitive insofar as it is performative, a speech that commands, that orders or assigns.

Indeed, after having quoted several verbs used in an equally transitive way by Trakl—"*schweigt*' ('silences'), '*blutet*' ('bleeds') in the poem 'An den Knaben Elis' and '*rauscht*' ('rustles') in the last line of 'Am Mönchsberg' ('By the Mönchsberg')"[37]— Heidegger signals as it were this commanding or assigning character that is addressed to the human by this *sprechen*. Last time we talked about performative speech as promise (*versprechen*), now here is performative speech as order or injunction. It appears in a sentence that plays on the relation between

36. Trakl, "Kaspar Hauser Lied," quoted in Heidegger, 75; "Kaspar Hauser Song," in *Poems and Prose*, 54/55.
37. Heidegger, 75.

Zusprechen, Zuspruch, and *Entsprechung*: *Zusprechen, Zuspruch* is consolation but also, and this isn't contradictory, exhortation, the encouraging to, the call to do something, etc., and *Entsprechung* is the corresponding, appropriate response, the cor-respondance, etc.

The sentence, then, defines God's speech, the sense and status of divine "*sprechen*" as transitive *sprechen* in the line from "Kaspar Hauser Lied,"

> Gott sprach eine sanfte Flamme zu seinem Herzen: O Mensch!"[38]

God's speech (*Gottes Sprechen*) is the *Zusprechen* [exhortation: the "mandate" ["*mandement*"] says the French translation] that assigns (*zuweist*) a quieter essence (*ein stilleres Wesen*) to the human being and, through this *Zusprechen, in die Entsprechung ruft* (calls him into a correspondence) toward which he, from out of proper decline (*aus dem eigentlichen Untergang*) *in die Frühe aufersteht* (he resurrects into the morning).[39]

The French translation says "*ressurgit*" ["resurges"] probably so as to avoid the Christian connotation of "*ressuscite*" ["resurrects"]; but *Auferstehung* is resurrection; and since the connotation could not be clearer or more inevitable in German, I don't see why one would avoid it in French. The problem of Trakl's Christianity: already seen.

We will return next time to conclude with this Heidegger text.

---

38. Trakl, "Kaspar Hauser Lied," quoted in Heidegger, 75; "Kaspar Hauser Song," in *Poems and Prose*, 54/55.

39. Heidegger, 75.

Thirteenth Session

This will be the last session before Easter, since I must go abroad [*à l'étranger*] starting tomorrow until the end of April.[1]

Travel, the foreign [*l'étranger*], indeed that's what we have been talking about since the beginning, not just the beginning of this seminar in general but since we have begun to read Trakl and Heidegger (*fremd, Fremdling, wandern, vorauswandern*). And then the return to the homeland, *Heimat,* to which we will return to conclude today, for this last session with Heidegger and for this last session before Easter. This Christian reading of Trakl, the very reading Heidegger wants to avoid at all costs, could very well bring everything back to Easter and even resurrection (*Auferstehung*), this word that the French translation sought to erase from the text by avoiding "*ressuscite*" ["resurrect"] for "*aufersteht,*" replacing it with "*ressurgit*" ["resurge"]. It is indeed a matter of resurrection, and to say that it is a matter

---

1. This last session of the seminar likely took place on March 20, 1985 (the first day of spring that year, as Derrida will point out below). The trip abroad to which Derrida refers here must have begun immediately after, since the conference at Loyola University, where he will present *Geschlecht II* and distribute the Loyola typescript—and, moreover, where he will speak of the "hundred or so pages" of the seminar he had then just concluded—took place March 22 to 23 in Chicago. This also explains why he did not have the time needed to transcribe the last five sessions of the seminar; see the preface, p. ix.

of thinking resurrection rather than of believing in it in a Christian way does not necessarily change all that much.

As for the return, a motif on which I very much insisted last time, this is the central theme of these last pages, which, incidentally, return toward their starting point, the first line quoted, "*Es ist die Seele ein Fremdes auf Erden.*" And this time the return is indeed a return toward what really must be translated into French as "*patrie*" ["homeland"] (*Heimat*), despite all the reservations we had to express about this Latin translation when Heidegger condemns or distances himself from "Patriotismus."[2]

Under the, let's say, very general heading of the "performative," I said at least three things last time.

1. One concerned the role of the promise (*Versprechen*) in the determination of the country [*das Land*, which is what promises dwelling] or in the announcement of the right strike, of sexual difference without fold, of the gentleness of peaceful difference in the morning, which is also a return (a messianic dimension Heidegger denies), and also the performative of the injunction or assignation of God's speech, of "*Gottes Sprechen*" as *Zusprechen*, and so on.

2. The other thing that pertained to the performative concerned what Heidegger, while discussing the return, makes of *das Land* and, as we shall see, of *Heimat*. The issue is that these themes are not merely themes, subject matters, objects. In his writing, in his manipulation and maneuvering of language, Heidegger's manner (Heidegger's hand) practices the return to the German idiom, to what links language to place, even if this place is not an empirical national territory. All the decisive and indispensable recourses to the German idiom—preferably Old and High German,—of the kind we noted so much of, attest to this return, the carrying out according to the step (*Schritt*) and hand (*Hand-Werk*)

2. See above, p. 34.

of the return to this *Heimat* we will be talking about, and which Heidegger speaks of, not merely to speak of it but in order to reach it, to get back to it. To reach home, that is the economy.

3. The third thing I link to this enigmatic performativity is what we are doing here by saying this, by choosing to study Heidegger, a Heidegger text on a poet, so slowly, so patiently, within a seminar on philosophical nationality and nationalism. Some would say—and this gives some idea of what we're doing here—that we are sketching out a comparatist practice. As I was saying last time, in our study of this Heidegger text we are interested not only in what Heidegger says, in his themes, his propositions on speech, Christianity, Platonism, sexual difference, history or the homeland, poetry or place, etc. We are observing his approach and his manner, how he does things, how he writes, proceeds, recedes, intercedes, and we are asking ourselves, as I did last time, why this approach and this manner, which is no longer even philosophical but which interrogates philosophy and deconstructs it from out of the *Gespräch* between thinking and poetry, why this approach has always been impossible anywhere other than in this Germany. And I repeat my request: if anyone among you can provide a counterexample, from another culture or another language, the example of an analogous attempt that is not tied to the German language and that does not suppose Heidegger's path-breaking, this would be of the utmost interest for the seminar.

I am imagining the impatience of some of you, not only with the emphatic slowness of this reading, but with the duration of this sojourn with Heidegger. Heidegger again! And this return of Heidegger, and this return to Heidegger! Isn't it enough already? Is this still topical?

To these questions, which I ask myself, as well, I will sketch out the following response. What interests me today is precisely the return of Heidegger and the return to Heidegger, and it is this that I also want to study. The Heidegger that returns or to which one returns is not the same as the one that made its appearance in France just before and just after the war, nor the one that reappeared again ten years later, when the first extensive translations and a new reading of Husserl, as well as the remove of the war, changed somewhat the space of his reception, as they say. And the Heidegger of today is still other, the political question being put to him is no longer the same, and the corpus that is available, now that his complete works are beginning to come out (wariness . . .) and new translations are at our disposal, this corpus has another configuration, and we glimpse new landscapes.

What I will call—without being sure of these words—the force, the necessity, but also the art of a thinking, is not measured by the duration and permanence of its radiant presence, it is not measured by the fixedness of a brightness, but by the number of its eclipses—and you see that in saying this we are continuing to speak within the text on Trakl, which is also a text on the year, the day, and the course of the sun. After each eclipse that this thinking is capable of enduring, it reappears again different as it emerges from the cloud, and the "same" text, the same legacy is no longer the same, it turns on itself and surprises us again. A thinker who does not accept the law of this eclipse and who does not calculate with it is not a thinker, he or she is at least a calculator who does not know how to calculate with the non-calculation that is the greatest risk, that of the eclipse without return, that of the absolute Stranger who does not come back.

What does this mean?

A question of memory, of technics and animality, here we are again. The "force" or "weakness" of a thinking is measured by its capacity for the strike (*Schlag*) and the double strike, that is, its capacity to inscribe itself in multiple places at once, to occupy multiple writing surfaces [*surfaces d'inscription*] that are so many memories. I will not say objective memories to refer to those types of memory that are books, computers, culture, the university, tradition, what Heidegger would also have called objective spirit, I won't speak of objective memory because it is precisely this value of objectivity that is questioned by what we are pondering from out of what Heidegger has left or bequeathed, the memories of which his text, his idiotext as <Bernard> Stiegler would say, occupies the writing surface. Every time, after an eclipse, something of his text imposes its reading upon us, reminds us of itself, reminds someone else, reminds others, in the very absence of Heidegger the subject (in a moment we will encounter these notions of subject and object, of the subject as object), this is because another writing surface, another textual power has been occupied in advance, and sufficiently bound to the idiom so as to seem unavoidable because it is untranslatable, but nevertheless translatable enough, calling out for translation enough to impose itself again paradoxically.

I am not imposing this question of memory, archive, legacy, and writing surfaces on the text that we are reading. Indeed, I am speaking of the memory capacity, a capacity both for inscribing and for retaining in memory. Every time after a night, the night of an eclipse, memory returns with a new text, as it were, when for example one realizes that in the same volume (a book, a page) multiple texts and thus multiple readings, multiple translations were inscribed, and that when one seems worn out, exhausted, the resource of another takes over (and this is how you can recognize the force or power of a text, by this accumulation of traces in the same volume, in the same engrammatic fold, by this elliptical or ecliptic economy), well this is indeed a question of a technics of memory. Now, Heidegger would like—and here we're coming back to his text, which stays with us—to dissociate two things, two times two things: on the one hand, technics and a certain thinking memory as two foreign essences; on the other hand, the animal and the human, the bestial animal and the human animal, the former having no memory, no thinking memory, the latter distinguishing itself by a certain force of thinking memory. These two oppositions or demarcations do not come down to the same thing, but they nevertheless cannot be dissociated. We were talking last week about technics and grasping reason as the realm of the *animal rationale* (*Vernunft, vernehmen*). You will recall that in the very beginning of the text it was a question of the animal that is or becomes the human through the memory it retains:

> Gedächte ein blaues Wild seines Pfads,
> Des Wohllauts seiner geistlichen Jahre![3]
> . . .
> Would that a blue game retained the memory of its path,
> Of the harmony of its spiritual years![4]

Further on, Heidegger asks:

> Who is this blue game which the poet enjoins [*zuruft*, orders, the performative again], this blue animal that would indeed be able to retain the memory of the stranger? An animal? Certainly. And only an animal? Not at all. For it is supposed to remember [. . .]. The blue game is an animal the animality of which does not presumably lie in bestiality (*im Tierischen*), but in that staring remembrance (*in jenem schauenden Gedenken*) for which the poet calls.[5]

It is on the basis of this thinking memory as *Gedenken* that Heidegger decides that this animal is thinking (*das denkende*), and the beginning of the *animal rationale*, but of an *animal rationale*

---

3. Trakl, "Sommersneige," quoted in Heidegger, "Die Sprache im Gedicht," 39.
4. Trakl, "Summer's Decline," in *Poems and Prose*, 94/95.
5. Heidegger, "Die Sprache im Gedicht," 41.

that is not yet secured in metaphysics, an *"animal rationale,*
the human [who], as Nietzsche puts it, has not yet been firmly
set (*fest gestellt*)."[6]

Naturally, it is this limit between two memories, as between the animal and the human, which is constantly called
into question in this seminar, and this is why I very much insisted on the question of animality before taking up this text.[7]
This question is also that of technics. But you've understood
that for me it is not a matter of effacing every limit or every
distinction between what one calls the beast and what one
calls the human, but rather of contesting the unity of this limit
as opposition on either side of a border that separates memory and non-memory, giving and taking—and memory is also
a kind of taking, keeping, seizing [*saisir*[8]], as one curiously
says today in the code of computers and "word processors"[9]:
one enters [*saisit*] a text, in French we say "*saisir un texte*" for
recording a text, putting it into objective memory in the ma-
chine or on the writing surface—thinking memory and biological memory, thinking memory and technological memory.
The differences between so-called animal species, including
the human, are very numerous (far more than one) and here
I'm speaking of structural differences in, let's say, engrammatic capacity and in the economy of inscription, let's say in
mnemonic power and structure.

And thus in the experience of territory.

And of sexual territory.

And of return, and of "homeland."

That said, and situated in the beginning, I will organize this
last session before Easter, which will also be the last devoted
to the final pages of the text on Trakl, around what comes

6. Heidegger, 41.

7. See Derrida, "Heidegger's Hand (*Geschlecht* II)."

8. In French, the word most commonly used for "entering" or "inputting"
data on a computer is "*saisir*," which primarily means "to grasp," "seize,"
or "understand." (—Trans.)

9. In English in the original. (—Trans.)

as it were at the center of this last part, namely, the motif of homeland and return. I'm thinking especially of a sentence that forms an entire paragraph on its own, and which says the following, I'm translating:

Trakl's poetry [*Trakls Dichtung*, difficult here to know if this is poetry in general or the poem "Occident" ("Abendland") or "Abendländisches Lied," which seems more likely to me] sings the song (*Gesang*) of the soul, which, "something strange on earth" ("*ein Fremdes auf Erden*"), first wanders and reaches the earth (*erst die Erde . . . erwandert*) as the quieter homeland of the homecoming *Geschlecht* [*des heimkehrenden Geschlechtes*, of the *Geschlecht* that reaches home].[10]

The calling of return and return to the house, to one's home, to home could not be more explicit. Homeland clearly does not have a national sense, in the usual modern and political meaning of the term, especially since it is a matter of a *Geschlecht* that is not limited to a defined nation. Nevertheless, as I said last time, it is a matter of a *Geschlecht* bound to an idiom, a place, and a land, and not of humanity in its abstract universality of a species, namely, in its ahistoricity.

And as it happens, the theme of history as such—in the difference between *Historie* and *Geschichte* or *Geschick* (destiny)—appears and appears only in the final pages of the text, precisely on the subject of the two poems "Occident" and "Occidental Song" (*Abendland* rather than Occident: already seen).

After having said that the *Sprechen* of God was a *Zusprechen* that enjoins the human to a quieter essence in order to resurrect "from out of the proper decline (*aus dem eigentlichen Untergang*) into morning," Heidegger gathers things together into this formulation, which picks up on the word *Untergang* as he quotes the title of the poem "Occident": "*Das 'Abendland' birgt den Aufgang der Frühe des 'Einen Geschlechts'* [The

10. Heidegger, "Die Sprache im Gedicht," 76.

Occident, 'Occident,' shelters the rise, *Aufgang, Auferstehen*, of the dawn of the '*One Geschlecht*']."[11] How are we to read this Occident? "How shortsighted would our thinking be were we to mean that the singer of 'Occidental Song' is a poet of the fall [*Verfall*, a word that appears in *Sein und Zeit*, however]." The *Untergang* of the evening is not the fall. Presupposing familiarity with the entire poem "Occident," with its three versions, even though he cites one line from the second version here (verified), and then, without warning, giving only the page numbers, a line from the third version, Heidegger suggests, "how muted [half, *halb*] and dull (*stumpf*) would our hearing be were we to cite only the last, third part of 'Occident,'" which is indeed very dark, and were we not to be attentive to what is found in "the center of the triptych" and at its beginning.[12]

The figure of Elis appears again in the poem "Occident," whereas "Helian" and "Sebastian im Traum" are no longer named in the last poems. The steps of the stranger resound [*tönen*, I imagine Heidegger is alluding to the line "*Oder es läuten die Schritte / Elis' durch den Hain* [. . .] *O des Knaben Gestalt*"[13]]. They are attuned (*sie sind gestimmt*) from out of the "quiet spirit" [*aus dem "liesen Geist*," a quote the quotation marks of which are lost in the French translation (still?), *leise*: sliding, discreetly] *der uralten Legende des Waldes* (of the ancient legend of the forest).[14]

This ancient legend of the forest is, it seems, that of the buried history of our country and in fact, in the lines I imagine Heidegger is alluding to, since he doesn't cite them, there is for example the "spirit of the forests" (*Geist der Wälder*), in a

11. Heidegger, 75.
12. Heidegger, 76.
13. Trakl, "Abendland," in *Das dichterische Werk*, 225; "The West," in *Poems and Prose*, 96/97.
14. Heidegger, "Die Sprache im Gedicht," 76.

stanza from the second version that starts with: "... *Hinstirbt der Väter Geschlecht* (dead race of fathers, or the sex of fathers)," and in the third stanza "*so leise sind die grünen Wälder / unserer Heimat.*"[15] These lines that are found in the third stanza of the second version, in the first line, are the very first line of the first version B (*Wanderschaft*).[16] Heidegger alludes to these lines, among other things, to mark a certain historicity of Trakl's poetry and its relation to the oldest origin of the homeland (*Heimat*), as well as to a certain historical becoming, since he also notes that the central part of the poem announces "the conclusion in which the 'big cities' ('*großen Städte*') are named, 'built with stones on the plain' [there he distorts the syntax of the line in order to quote it]."[17] In question is the second stanza of the fifth part (of the second version), which says:

> Groß sint Städte aufgebaut
> *Und steinern in der Ebene* [and the following line says:]
> *Aber es folgt der Heimatlose* (but follows the one without
> homeland).[18]

These cities, this civilization of modernity and urban dwelling thus has its fate sealed:

> These big cities already have their *Schicksal* [this is conferred upon them, sent or assigned to them]. This is another destiny than the one spoken in the "verdant hill" [another quotation] where the "spring storm resounds," the hill to which a "just measure" ("*gerechtes Maß*") is proper [implied: excessiveness and monstrosity are on the side of the great

15. Trakl, "Abendland," 221.
16. Trakl, 220.
17. Heidegger, "Die Sprache im Gedicht," 76.
18. Trakl, "Abendland," 224.

cities of stone], and which is also called the *"Abendhügel"* ["evening hill," where we find the entire hesperal, occidental thematics we were talking about].[19]

This insistence on the homeland, the very ancient legend of the forests, the loss of measure that characterizes urban modernity, in order to recall that Trakl is attentive to a certain historicity and that this evaluation of the relation between forest and city is not, as one might believe, a refuge from history, precisely. "One has spoken [Heidegger recalls] of Trakl's *'innerster Geschichtlosigkeit,'* [of his 'innermost lack of history']. But what does *'Geschichte'* mean in this judgment?"[20] This noun is then understood not in its sense (*Geschichte*: history as that which happens, if you will, *geschehen*) but in the (Latin, again) sense of *Historie*, "that is, as representation of the past (*das Vorstellen des Vergangenen*)."[21] *Historie*, history as the historian's activity, the realm of representative narrative, a bustle about historical "objects," does not give the measure of historicity in the sense of *Geschichte*. "Trakl's poetizing has no need of historiographical 'objects,'" nor of this representation (*Vorstellen*).[22] The modern and metaphysical objection to Trakl's supposed ahistoricity stems from this objectivism and this philosophy of representation that is the mark of post-Cartesian modernity. I note in passing that what the French translation renders as "historical subjects" [*"sujets historiques"*] in the sentence "His poetizing [Trakl's] has no need of historical 'subjects,'" what we must understand as objects (*Gegenstände*), subjects in the sense of themes, content, etc.

Why does Trakl not need historical objects to represent? "Because his poem is *geschichtlich* [historical, historial] in the

19. Heidegger, "Die Sprache im Gedicht," 76.
20. Heidegger, 76.
21. Heidegger, 76.
22. Heidegger, 76.

highest sense." What does this height consist of, this high content, this historial high quality? What does this event-ness, this advent-ness of Trakl's poetry? For if it is *geschichtlich*, this is because it is not content with showing or representing historical objects, it makes history and destiny happen, it is in itself the event, something of the event that it speaks, or that it sings, rather, for it is the song that here overflows or precedes the *Vorstellen*, the representation of historical objects. One could speak here of a sort of performativity of the poetic song that is not content with representing historical objects for historians but which is historial insofar as it moves, stirs, promotes events. In any case, what it sings are not representations of what happens, objects, but happening itself, the coming of what comes. And as the song is not an objective representation from afar, it is right up next to, it attends at the birth of that which comes. Here we must read closely the sentence in which Heidegger explains, as it were, in what sense "Trakl's *Gedicht* is *geschichtlich* in the highest sense." I will first read the German:

> *Seine Dichtung singt das Geschick des Schlages, der das Menschengeschlecht in sein noch vorbehaltenes Wesen verschlägt, d. h. rettet* [His poetry sings the *Geschick* (sending and destiny, the dispensation (French translation: "*mission*"), what is assigned, signified but in the gesture of sending, *schicken*, destining, addressing; so his poetry sings the missing—hear "mission" in the sense of an emission that sends and destines) of the strike (des *Schlages*, the blow, the mark, the blow or the mark are sent, addressed)].[23]

In sum—I'm interrupting my translation to underscore this—this means that it is pointless and impossible and illegitimate to think *Geschichtlichkeit*, historiality, the being historical of history in its event-ness (before all representation) if one does

23. Heidegger, 76.

not start from something like sending, and sending as the sending of the mark, strike, blow: in the beginning, sending and the
sending of a mark. This mark or this sending of the mark is a
gift that comes, I will say without glossing Heidegger in this particular text, but in agreement with what he suggests elsewhere
(ZS²⁴), a gift that comes before being itself (. . .). So, let me
continue the translation of the same sentence: "His poetry
sings [stress] the destinal sending of the mark [strike, blow,
stamp] which *verschlägt* [which strikes by separating, by "specifying" ["*spécifiant*"] says the French translation] [. . .]";²⁵
and indeed, it is a question of a strike which sets apart, which
separates but in order to give it its specificity, its originality, its proper mark, its properness, its specific propriety,
one could also say its idiomaticity: to what? What strikes
what with specificity? Well, the *Menschengeschlecht*, the strike
strikes with its proper stamp the *Menschengeschlecht*, it causes
it to become a *Geschlecht*, *Menschengeschlecht*, it is the origin of the human species, of what is proper to man as such,
it writes humanity, it inscribes humanity, it imprints humanity as such, it imprints upon it its mark and imprints upon it
its movement, gives it (to) being [*lui donne à être*], makes it
happen. There is not first the *Menschengeschlecht* that then
receives this stamp; no, the *Menschengeschlecht*, the proper
of man and the sexuality of the species happen from out of
this strike. What, then, could be more historial (*geschichtlich*),
if not historical, than this strike? What event, what advent,
more "vent-like" ["*vènementiel*"]? What higher vent-ness [*vène-
mentalité*]? What can happen, occur, *geschehen* that is higher?
Nonetheless, this historiality, this *Geschichtlichkeit* is not historical (*historisch*, if you will) in the sense that it does not lend itself

24. "ZS" may refer here to "Zeit und Sein," in *Zur Sache des Denkens*
(*GA* 14), ed. Friedrich-Wilhelm von Herrmann (1969; Frankfurt am Main:
Vittorio Klostermann, 2007). Published in English as Martin Heidegger,
On Time and Being, trans. Joan Stambaugh (Chicago: University of Chicago
Press, 2002).

25. Heidegger, "Die Sprache im Gedicht," 76.

to the objective representation of historians, it cannot be told like a story or a historical subject.

I have not yet commented on the last word, no doubt the most unusual and most difficult word. That is to say, says Heidegger "[. . .] *verschlägt, d.h. rettet* [strikes with difference, that is to say, saves, saves] the *Menschengeschlecht*."[26] This strike saves what is proper to man, that on account of which he is more historial than any historian's history, than any historical representation. This salvation is at once arche-originary—because it is a question of the strike that gives humanity its proper stamp and makes it come into itself, into its essence, saving it from what it is not or must not be—at once archeoriginary and to come (in keeping with the open circle we were talking about the last times). To come, still a promise, I'm hardly daring in saying messianism, to the extent that the sentence says of this essence, of this being (*Wesen*) in which the *Menschengeschlecht* is struck, stamped with difference, that it is this essential being "*in sein noch vorbehaltenes Wesen* [still reserved being, held in reserve in advance, enveloped in a kind of reserved secret, awaiting its future, promised, in short]."[27]

Being is promised, a promise of itself. And only this promise, this stamp of the promise imprinted with a strike in the essence of the human, can also save the *Geschlecht*. There is no difference, no distance or distinction, no temporal interval between *verschlagen* and *retten*: to strike with difference and to save. "*Verschlägt, d.h. rettet:*" "the sending of the strike (*das Geschick des Schlages*) that strikes with difference, *that is to say*, saves the *Menschengeschlecht* into its still reserved essence [its promise]."[28] What is important here is the "that is to say" that connects and harmonizes the strike with salvation as the same historial event, arche-originary and to come.[29] This

26. Heidegger, 76.
27. Heidegger, 76.
28. Heidegger, 76 (Derrida's emphasis).
29. Marginal addition: "*salvation* can come in one blow."

"that is to say" is not said by the poet, it is sung. For, all of this, everything we have just read and translated is what "*seine Dichtung singt* (what Trakl's poetry sings)." But since by singing it does not tell or relate stories or historical objects from the past, it does not represent, one may say that by singing it strikes and saves, it participates in the event that it sings, it summons the strike that saves.

This unison of the sung "that is to say," this song of an arche-origin that strikes with or from the future that is also promise and salvation, this indeed takes the form of a return. The movement toward the future is a return toward the arche-origin.

That is to say, toward the homeland, *Heimat* or *Land, das Land* being what promises, precisely, what promises dwelling but dwelling as that toward which one always returns. The return is not an accidental or supplementary predicate of dwelling or the homeland (*Heimat*), it is the essential movement that originarily constitutes or institutes the homeland or country as a promise of dwelling. The country begins with the promise of return. The country, as homeland (*Heimat*), is not a place one originally inhabited and toward which, one day, having left it, one desires to return. The country (*Land* or *Heimat*) appears as such only from out of the promise of return, even if, de facto, one has never left it, and even if, de facto, one never has to get back to it. It is in this way that the originary country announces itself, as it were: in the return as promise, the promised return which is also necessarily and irreducibly the return of the promise. That's what is sung, and it is immediately following this sentence about the strike of difference as salvation and promise of salvation—and the promise is already salvation: event of the promise itself (comment)—it is immediately following this "that is to say," "*verschlägt, d.h. rettet*," that the sentence I quoted a few minutes ago, which I said was at the center of this third part, comes, after a line break:

Trakl's poetry sings the song [*Gesang*: *Gedicht*] of the soul, which, "something strange on earth" ("*ein Fremdes auf Erden*"), first wanders and reaches the earth (*erst die Erde . . . erwandert*) as the quieter homeland (*als die stillere Heimat*) *des heimkehrenden Geschlechtes* [of the returning *Geschlecht*, making its return, coming home, *heimkehrend*, homecoming].[30]

Heidegger defends himself then in the face of the reaction he imagines: this is a romantic dream that takes refuge in this arche-origin to which he wants to return with the nostalgia of the lost homeland, the lost country, a nostalgia that keeps him at a distance from technological modernity and the progress of mass civilization, "mass existence" (*Massendasein*), in short, from what one calls the future. It is not about that. Lucidity about the future is on the side of this madman Trakl speaks of, on the side of the "clear knowing of this 'madman' (*das klare Wissen des 'Wahnsinnigen'*)" who sees something entirely different from the journalists, reporters of the so-called news [*actualité*], or those who exhaust themselves in stories, history (*Historie*, precisely), the representation of the present, of the now, of the now present object (*des Gegenwärtigen*).[31] These reporters, these journalists, these historians, these men of representation and present objectvity see neither the present nor the future, or at least they see a present that is only the object of representation and a future that is not the future because it is only the calculating, calculated projection, without any new event, without other, the programmed prolongation of current events [*l'actualité*], the extension of current events. This future of calculation and programming is not a future, *Zukunft*:

[. . .] because it remains without the arrival (*Ankunft*) [of some sending, here the French translation is very bad, it loses in particular the *Zukunft/Ankunft* relation] of a destiny

30. Heidegger, "Die Sprache im Gedicht," 76.
31. Heidegger, 76.

[something given or bestowed to share, without destiny, *Geschick*] which concerns human beings ["concern" is *angehen*] in the inception (*Anbeginn*) of their essence?[32]

Nothing arrives to human beings with this calculable programming of the future that only extends current events. And nothing arrives to them except for what seems to arrive in this way, the events reported by journalists and historians, because this does not concern being and the origin, the destination of the human. The future, which is not separable from this original destination, is not on the side of these supposed historical and journalistic current events, on the side of this objective and subjective representation. The future, what can come and arrive, is on the side of what Trakl sings, at the very moment one accuses him of being indifferent to historicity (distinguish between two historicities, *Historie, Geschichte, Geschick*, etc., and comment).

The end of the text is no doubt a general repetition of everything that has been said, a gathering (*Versammlung*), precisely, with the return of the first line of poetry quoted, "*Es ist die Seele ein Fremdes auf Erden*," which in this clever loop now finds itself reinserted into its poem.

(Describe the gesture, composition, manner: quotation of the line on its own (a reading over the course of more than 40 pages) and, to conclude, reinsertion of the line in the poem "Frühling der Seele," one of the two that bear this title and which is collected in *Sebastian im Traum*. Heidegger does not quote the entire poem but the last stanza in which the line is found.)

As for this final send-off, I will quickly emphasize, in conclusion, a certain number of features:

1. It is on the poem "Frühling der Seele," from which the line "*Es ist die Seele . . .*" is taken, that the conclusion of the text closes or rather opens; the springtime (first time, *primus*,

32. Heidegger, 76.

beginning of the year, *Jahr, gehen,* first of the seasons) that begins between March 19 and 21, so, this very day—and, calculating as I am, I programmed everything so that the final session of this seminar which was dedicated to this text that ends with an opening and a send-off onto spring, and onto the journey, so that the final session of this reading of "Frühling der Seele," of Trakl and Heidegger reading Trakl and situating this springtime, this opening at the end, so that this final session would fall, as they say, on the first day of spring, on the eve of Easter and a journey to the new world.

Frühling is indeed the moment of what comes the earliest, and *früh* is the word that *orients,* the Orient of the text, and every time one translates *früh,* the adjective or the noun (*Frühe*) as early, matutinal, originary, etc., without marking its link with the season, with the German word for spring (*Frühling*), one loses an essential thread of the text, or renders it in any case hardly visible.

2. This *Frühling* that comes at the end because it is at the beginning (according to the anniversary, the turning of the year, the revolution of the seasons) is, then, the opening of the year, and it transfigures death or mourning into promise and salvation of the future. This is why Heidegger recalls again his distinction between *Verfall* and *Untergang* (*Verfall* and *Sein und Zeit,* comment, necessity of the fall but . . .). The soul, something strange on earth, is sent, destined, sent off down a trail (*Pfad*)—the trail it follows— which does not lead to a fall (*Verfall*) but to that decline or inclination that leads to the morning, *in der Frühe,* or to the spring. And death itself, let's say that being-toward-death of the young man, is a death to which "this decline bows and complies":

This decline bows and complies to the powerful dying
[the prodigious, powerful, extraordinary, violent,

*gewaltig*³³] which [very difficult to translate] *der in der Frühe Verstorbene vorstirbt* [the dying that the one who has died dies in advance, *vorstirbt*, "dies by showing the way" ["*meurt en montrant la voie*"], says the French translation, pre-dies, dies not only prematurely but in anticipation, the one who has died, *Verstorbene, in der Frühe*, the morning, in, let's say, the spring, in the springtime, in the primeness of time].³⁴

Death in this springtime: not, I would say, that someone dies in the spring at a particular time, a particular moment, but his death, this death is the springtime, what arrives, what comes and returns from the future.

3. This arrives only with the song; it can only be called, and be called with the song, be called because it belongs to the promise (it is not a fact or a given) and be called with the song, because it is an essential event of the *Sprache* (*Dichten* and essence of *Sprache*) that is entwined, if you will, with the intonation and transitive silence we have spoken of. But who sings this song and who calls this death? It is the brother, it is the brother who dies in this powerful (*gewaltig*) way, powerful because, discreetly, it accomplishes, it does something, first it sings and the song does not describe, does not say what is, does not record, it calls and thereby makes arrive and come. It is the brother, then, who sings, he is also the poet who dies this death, who accomplishes this death in accordance with the spring, who "knows" how to sing and die as one must . . . The brother, who is the singing one (*der singende*), dies by following that decline that is not the fall, "*Ihm stirbt der Bruder als der singende nach.*"³⁵ It is not the selenic sister.

33. Marginal addition: "Quotation." This refers to a line from Trakl: "*Gewaltiges Sterben und die singende Flamme im Herzen*" (Trakl, "Frühling der Seele," 77). The word "*gewaltig*" is circled in the typescript.

34. Heidegger, "Die Sprache im Gedicht," 76.

35. Heidegger, 77.

Dying [*ersterbend*, difficult to translate, like all those *sterben* words: *Verstorbene, vorsterben, ersterben*, which have more or less the same meaning], and following the stranger, the friend stays over the spiritual night of the years of departedness (*Abgeschiedenheit*).[36]

Heidgger then follows the passage with a blackbird from the "Song of a Captive Blackbird" ("Gesang einer gefangenen Amsel") dedicated to Ludwig von Ficker. "The blackbird is the bird that calls Elis to his *Untergang* (decline)."[37] (continue)

There would naturally be much to say, taking into account "Ein *Geschlecht*," this one of one sex, one species in the simplicity of its difference, there would be much to say from this point of view about the fact that the figure of the brother is the only one who gathers this song together: neither the sister, nor anyone else (neither father, nor mother, son, or daughter). Would this mean that all these "familial" figures are figures that specify the brother, that not only the father and the son are brothers, which seems a bit obvious, but that the mother, daughter and sister are also brothers and that, above all, those who do not belong to the generic or genealogical family are brothers, the brother thus marking the rupture with the familial structure—rupture, escape, or emancipation, the friend following the brother? (Figure of the homeland or beyond the homeland in fraternity? Natality, naturality, nationality, or the opposite, or its beyond?) A question that I leave suspended. Heidegger reminds us, incidentally, in conclusion, of the danger of set formulations. These are always of the order of the exteriority of opinion, of doxa (good for reporters, etc.) but they help us nevertheless, he concedes, and what's at stake is his concluding formulation on Trakl's situation:

36. Heidegger, 77.
37. Heidegger, 77.

A situation (*Erörterung*) of his *Gedicht* shows us Georg
Trakl [so named: him and not another, and not Heidegger,
not the generality of an era] as the poet *des noch verborgenen
Abend-Landes.*

And then, just as he had begun by quoting without saying anything beforehand, at the beginning of the first part, so here
he quotes at length to conclude without saying anything af-
terwards. He quotes, then, the stanza that encircles the line
quoted in the first place. I will read it, a bit in both languages,
without adding anything in turn. Read.

> Dunkler umfließen die Wasser die schönen Spiele der
>   Fische.
> Stunde der Trauer, schweigender Anblick der
>   Sonne;
> Es ist die Seele ein Fremdes auf Erden. Geistlich
>   dämmert
> Bläue über dem verhauenen Wald und es läutet
> Lange eine dunkle Glocke im Dorf; friedlich Geleit.
> Stille blüht die Myrthe über den weißen Lidern des
>   Toten.
>
> Leise tönen die Wasser im sinkenden Nachmittag
> Und es grünet dunkler die Wildnis am Ufer, Freude im
>   rosigen Wind;
> Der sanfte Gesang des Bruders am Abendhügel.
> . . .
> Darker the waters flow about the lovely games of the
>   fish.
> Hour of mourning, silencing glance of the sun;
> It is, the soul, something strange on earth. Spiritually in
>   twilight
> Blue upon the clear-cut forest, and in the village
> A dark bell tolls long; peaceful procession.

Quietly myrtle blossoms above the white eyelids of the
  dead.

Softly resound the waters in the falling afternoon,
And the wilderness grows green more darkly by the
  shore; joy in the rosy wind;
The gentle song of the brother on the evening hill.[38]

38. Trakl, "Springtime of the Soul II," in *Poems and Prose*, 98/99.

INDEX

Gedicht (*cont.*)
indivisibility of, 80–81, 88; place
of Trakl's, 14, 26–29, 50, 52, 56,
70, 75–77, 84, 88, 103, 114; translation of, 19–20; as unspoken,
13, 20–21, 23, 27, 35, 51, 70–71,
75–76, 85, 88
German
Germanity, xxiii–xxv, xxvii, 100–
102, 136
language, xxi–xxiv, xxvi–xxvii,
3n3, 4, 15, 21–22, 30, 48, 58,
99, 114, 116, 134–36, 138, 141,
156; *Geschlecht* and, xi; Heidegger's, xxix, 2n2, 133; idiom,
xxi, xxviii, 15, 23, 140; Old High,
xviii, xxix, 30, 32–34, 50, 57–
58, 65, 68, 75–76, 106, 140; as
"our language," xxi, 105; relation to Latin, 77
nation, xxi–xxii, 99–100
nationalism, xxi–xxx, 99–101
national-philosophism, xxviii
people, xxii–xxv;
philosophy, xxv, xxviii–xxix
Germany, xxix, 100, 134–37, 141
Geschlecht: animality and, 29; decomposing or decomposed form
of, xxx, 44–46, 50, 53, 63–64;
definitions of, viii, xi, 4n5, 45,
47–48; as "family," 98; family
of, xviii, 47; in Fichte, xxii–xxix;
as "generation," 67–68; in Heidegger, xi, xv, 4n5, 5, 44, 61, 75,
84, 154; as "humanity" or "human essence," xxi, xxviii, 4n5,
45; *Menschengeschlecht*, xxii,
xxvi, 45, 65, 129, 151–52; "one"
(*Ein*) xxix–xxx, 27, 75–76, 93,
120, 122–29, 131, 137, 145, 147,
158; polysemy of, 126; relation
to place, 146; relation to *Schlag*,
xviii, 9n10, 31, 45–49, 52, 121, 131,
137, 151; scene of, 67; as "sex," xvi,

xviii–xix, 9n10, 45–47, 63–67, 82;
as "species," 45–48, 53, 63, 66; as
theme or title of Derrida work,
vii–x, xiii, xvii, xx, 3; to come,
69, 91, 103, 152; in Trakl, 46, 122,
148; translatability of, viii, xi,
xxii–xxiv, 48; as word or mark,
xi, 3n3, 5, 127
"*Geschlecht I*, Sexual Difference,
Ontological Difference" (Derrida), viiin2, xii, xiv–xv, xvii–
xviii, xx, 3, 47n113
Ghost of the Other, The (1984–85
Derrida seminar), ix, xx–xxi,
xxvin33, xxix, xxxi, 51
Glas (Derrida), xiiin9, 54, 90
Goethe, Johann Wolfgang von, 96,
101–2
Grün, Karl Theodor Ferdinand,
xxviii
Grundton, 27, 73, 75–76, 82, 124–25

Hegel, Georg Wilhelm Friedrich,
xii, xxviii, 44, 54–55, 66, 82, 90,
93, 102, 115, 119
Heidegger, Martin: difficulty in
translating (see "translation");
manner of reading of, 1–2, 5–16,
18–19, 21–29, 35–39, 43, 51, 56,
59–63, 70, 88, 121–25, 140–41;
motif of gathering (see "gathering"); nationalism of, xxix–xxx,
77; political and sexual themes
in, xi; relation to Christianity
(see "Christianity"); relation to
German language (see "German
language"); relation to National
Socialism, xxix–xxx; "situation"
of Trakl (see "*Erörterung*" and
"*Gedicht*"); as subject of Derrida's *Geschlecht* series, vii–xi, xx;
as subject of Derrida's seminar,
139–43; thinking of animality (see
"animality"); thinking of country

or homeland (see "country" and "homeland"); thinking of humanity (see "human"); thinking of idiom (see "idiom"); thinking of language (see *Sprache*); thinking of place (see "place"); thinking of polysemy (see "polysemy" and "dissemination"); thinking of sexual difference, xiii–xix, 43, 45–47, 69, 125–29; thinking of spirit (see "spirit"); thinking of the West (see "West, the"); thought of, 3, 4n5
"Heidegger's Hand (*Geschlecht* II)" (Derrida), viin1, viii–x, xvii, xx, xxix, 14n21, 40n89, 112, 139n1, 145n7
"Heidegger's Ear, Philopolemology (*Geschlecht IV*)" (Derrida), viii, x
Heimatlosigkeit, 98, 101
Hitler, Adolf, xxix
Hölderlin, Friedrich, 40n90, 95–102, 108, 134
homeland, 41, 74, 101, 145–46, 149, 158; as *Heimat*, 97–99, 132, 139–41, 148, 153–54
human/humanity, xxi–xxii, xxvi–xxvii, 4n5, 6n6, 11n16, 25, 64–65, 69, 98, 101, 107, 115, 119, 128, 131, 137–38, 151–59; as *animal rationale*, 40–42, 116; as one definition of "*Geschlecht*," xi, 45; decomposed form of (see "*Geschlecht*"); European, 100; relation to the animal, 144–46
humanism, xxvii, xxix–xxx, 96–97, 101–2, 115
Hume, David, xxviii
Husserl, 74, 100–101, 142

idiom, xxi, 3n3, 15, 16n26, 23–24, 30, 53, 55, 76, 130, 151; as absolute, 56; German, xxi, xxviii, 23, 30, 57–58, 76, 133, 140; *Geschlecht*

as, 48, 146; Heideggerian, 64, 133; importance for Heidegger's reading, xxix, 54, 61, 140; as national, xxi, xxvii–xxviii, 32; and poetry, 19–20; in relation to place, 11, 19, 22; as secret, xxi; as untranslatable, 52, 57–59, 143; Indo-European, 38, 59

Jankélévitch, Samuel, xxiii

Kant, Immanuel, xxviii, 55
Kierkegaard, Søren, 85
Krell, David F., viin1, xxxiv

Latin language, xxvi, 25, 32, 34, 59, 68, 77–78, 98–99, 105–6, 117, 134, 140, 149
Letter on Humanism (Heidegger), 96–97, 101–2
Levinas, Emmanuel, xii
"Loyola typescript," ix–x, xviii, xxxi–xxxiii, 50

Marburg lecture course (Heidegger), xvi, xviii, 3, 47
Marx, xxviii, 101
metonymy, 27, 35–36, 38–39, 56–57, 61, 89
McDonald, Christie, xii, xiv
Michelet, Jules, xxviii
morning, 10, 61, 63, 68–69, 114–15, 119, 131–32, 138, 140, 146, 156–57

nationalis: biological-racial, xxi, xxiii, xxix–xxx; Fichtean, xxi–xxix; German, xxi–xxx, 99–102; in Heidegger, 77, 99–102, 115–16, 131–34; philosophical, xxi–xxix, 95, 131–32, 141; relation to humanism, xxvii
Nazism, xxvii–xxviii
Nietzsche, Friedrich, 6n6, 40–41, 62, 98, 113, 116–17, 119, 145